Diving Complete

Diving Complete

GEORGE RACKHAM

FABER AND FABER LTD
3 Queen Square London

First published in 1975
by Faber and Faber Limited
3 Queen Square London WC1
Filmset and printed in Great Britain by
BAS Printers Limited, Wallop, Hampshire
All rights reserved

ISBN 0 571 10342 1 (hard covers)
ISBN 0 571 10940 3 (paper covers)

Contents

Photographs

Photographs 2, 3, 4, 22, 23, 24, 25 and 27 are reproduced by kind permission of Tony Duffy

All line illustrations are by the author.

Acknowledgement

My grateful thanks to my wife for her
assistance in checking the manuscript and for
her forbearance, encouragement and patience,
without which this book would not have been
possible.

Preface

This book has been written to assist the growing number of diving enthusiasts. It is the result of knowledge and experience gained in the teaching, coaching and lecturing field over a period of many years.

Chapters 1 to 12 deal mainly with the teaching progressions, covering the introduction to diving, and continuing on to the basic dives from the springboard. These practices will enable anyone to teach diving to the most unlikely candidate. These chapters should prove of great assistance to teachers of school-children. It will enable them to make diving a valuable addition to the physical education programme.

The number of learner pools available to schools is increasing each year. The teacher will find that the exercises outlined in Chapter 5, 'First Steps in Diving', will provide material that will not only introduce variety into the swimming lesson, but will also allow the necessary diving preparation to be taught at the desirable early stage.

A chapter on the history of diving is included to provide the diving enthusiast with a suitable background, and to give an insight into how the sport has evolved to reach its present level of sophistication. Chapter 3, 'Safety', provides answers to the many questions posed by the diving teacher and will give greater confidence in teaching and also help to prevent possible accidents to the pupils.

Chapters 13 to 22 deal with the techniques used in the execution of the various dives. In these chapters I have tried to explain as simply as possible 'how and why', suggesting various practical experiments that will provide a greater appreciation of the mechanical principles involved. Armed with this knowledge, it is possible for a non-diving teacher to teach and coach diving to quite a high level of performance.

If this book does nothing more than remove some of the mystique and ignorance surrounding the sport, it will have achieved its purpose. Coaches will find much food for thought in these chapters, in which, if approached with an open mind, many of the difficulties associated with the more complex somersaulting and twisting dives will resolve themselves, leaving a clearer understanding of what is necessary to achieve a desired result.

GEORGE RACKHAM
London 1975

1. *History*

No sport has altered so much during its history as diving. During the early nineteenth century the only references to it in the books on swimming referred to a simple plunge from the side as a means of entering the water for the purpose of swimming. This was eventually developed and performed for its own sake and became known as 'plunging'. In 1893 the first Plunging Championship was inaugurated. The English Amateur Record of 86 feet 8 inches (26.4 metres) was made by F. W. Parrington at Bootle in 1933. The Plunging Championship continued until 1937.

The Evolution of Diving Diving for its own sake had already developed from the plunge, and the take-off was being attempted from greater heights as these became available. Many of the early divers were gymnasts who found a new and exciting way of indulging in gymnastic feats with less chance of injury. Eventually the entry into the water became for these enthusiasts just a landing medium and the take-off and flight through the air became the 'dive'. This difference caused some confusion in the swimming world, and Ralph Thomas, the noted swimming historian, urged the adoption of the term 'springing' to apply to entering the water from an elevation. By this time however the word 'dive' had become so firmly established that it was too late to change it.

Diving was fast becoming a separate sport with its own devotees. It needed courage, a spirit of daring and the will to persevere in spite of the numerous smacks received when attempting to dive from greater heights.

The main problem with jumping and diving from heights in those days was finding suitable places. People began jumping from bridges in Europe and the U.S.A. and later diving in head first from them. Indians in Acapulco, Mexico, were adept at jumping and diving from high cliffs into the sea. Visitors to Hawaii in the late nineteenth century, recounted how the natives leaped, dived and somersaulted from considerable heights. This was often done into deep pools at the bottom of waterfalls for the sheer fun and excitement it provided. In England, harbours and piers at seaside resorts became favourite rendezvous for the new sport.

Development of Diving in Europe At the beginning of the nineteenth century a new form of diving was developing in Europe, mainly in Germany and Sweden where formal gymnastics were popular. During the summer months, gymnastic apparatuses were transferred to the beach where exercise out of doors was the vogue. The flying rings, trapeze and springboard were erected and used from high platforms to enable gymnastics over the water to be performed, using the water as a more comfortable landing medium than the less yielding gymnasium floor. This was the beginning of 'fancy diving' the name later given to aerial acrobatics over the water. Until this time, most diving was 'plain' diving in the form of the simple forward header with the body held straight and arms extended sideways, known in the early days in Europe as the 'Swedish Swallow' and later in the U.S.A. as the 'Swan Dive'.

Plate 1. Helen Koppel *A.S.A. Springboard and Highboard Champion 1973: Forward Dive Straight, 10 metre*

The trapeze and rings were gradually discarded and diving from platform and springboard incorporating gymnastic somersaults developed as a separate sport (with its own devotees) and became known as Springboard Diving and Fancy High Diving.

Prior to the First World War, Sweden dominated the Plain and Fancy High Diving events. In both the 1908 and 1912 Olympic Games,

Swedish men divers won the bronze, silver and gold medals in the Plain High Diving, and in the first Fancy High Diving event in the 1912 Games, they won the gold and bronze with Germany taking the silver. In the women's Plain High Diving event held for the first time in 1912, the Swedes took first and second places with Belle White of Great Britain third. The men's Springboard events in the Olympic Games prior to the First World War were dominated by the German divers who won all bronze, silver and gold medals. The one exception was the U.S.A. diver, Sheldon, who won the Springboard event at the St. Louis (U.S.A.) Games in 1904. European Championships were introduced in 1926 under the jurisdiction of the LEN (European Swimming League) to take place in between the Olympic years. With the U.S.A. divers not eligible, this event provided a wonderful stimulus for the European divers. Germany dominated these events winning more medals than any other nation. Britain's only golds were Betty Slade (Springboard) in 1938 at the Wembley Empire Pool, London, and Brian Phelps who, at the age of fourteen, won the Highboard event with ease in 1958 at Budapest. He repeated his success in 1962 at Leipzig. 1966 saw the Italian diver Klaus Dibiasi win the gold medal with Phelps in second place.

The Plain Dive   The term 'Plain Dive' was given to all dives performed running or standing in which the diver took off facing the water and entered head first without any intermediate somersaults or twists. During the flight, the body was not allowed to be piked or hunched as these were regarded as Fancy Dives. The first divers in this country performed a Plain Dive with the arms held above the head during the flight, later to become known as the English Header. However, the early Plain Diving competitions were always won by the Swedish divers who demonstrated their beautiful Swedish Swallow. The English Header soon lost favour as it was more difficult to control than the Swallow and it eventually disappeared from competitive diving. All running Swallow Dives were performed from a one-foot take-off, as it was considered that this gave more control than a take-off from two feet. Divers today may find it difficult to appreciate the position the Swallow Dive held prior to the First World War. Fancy Diving was in its infancy and the Swallow reigned supreme. Each part of the dive was described in great detail. It was aesthetically pleasing to watch, something that cannot be said for many of the complex twisting somersaulting dives that make up the modern competitive diving programme.

Plain Diving in Great Britain   In 1889 the first diving proper championship took place in Scotland. It included a dive from a height of about 6 feet (1.8 m). In 1893 the first diving stage in England was erected at the Highgate Pond (London). It was a firm board fixed at a height of about 15 feet (4.6 m) above the surface. In 1895 the Royal Life Saving Society staged the first National Graceful Diving Competition, open to the world at Highgate Pond. It was for men only and comprised standing and running Plain Dives from heights of 15 feet (4.6 m) and 33 feet (10 m). The 10 metre stage was a temporary structure fitted up each summer for a few weeks and taken down after the competition. This competition was handed over to the Amateur Diving Association in 1920 and taken over by the A.S.A. in 1935 and renamed the Plain Diving Championship. Until 1953 it was held outdoors at various holiday resorts, but in 1954 it was transferred to the indoor Derby Bath at Blackpool where it continued until 1961 when the competition was discontinued. The Plain Diving competition, devoted entirely to the Swallow Dive, had survived unchanged for over sixty years. Plain Diving was introduced into the Olympic Games programme for the first time in 1904 at St. Louis, U.S.A. and it continued as a separate event until 1924.

Fancy High Diving   In the late 'nineties Messrs. Johansson, Hagberg and Mauritzi came over from Sweden and demonstrated the art of 'Fancy High Diving' from the 10 metre platform erected at Highgate Pond. This resulted in the formation of the Amateur Diving Association in 1901, the first official organization in the world devoted to the sport of diving. There were more facilities for platform diving in Europe than in the U.S.A. and the European divers from England or Northern Europe dominated the Plain Diving events. In England and most of Europe divers graduated from Plain Diving, taking off from platforms, to Fancy Diving from platforms, then to springboards. In the U.S.A., diving started later and grew up via springboard diving. The definition of Fancy Diving was 'dives with somersaults or twists'. 'Fancy' Dives were included for the first time in competition in 1903. Springboard diving was included in the Olympic Games at St. Louis in 1904. In the 1928 Olympics the men's Plain and Fancy High Diving events were amalgamated into one competition and renamed Highboard Diving and the word 'Fancy' disappeared from diving vocabulary.

The Evolution of the Body Positions   In the early 1920s most Fancy Dives were performed in the straight position from both spring and firm boards. The Amateur Diving Association (England) stated in 1921 that: 'Certain somersaults may be made with a bend at the hips and knees if the board is not sufficiently high to allow the limbs to be kept straight. "Back Front" dives should be performed with no bend at the hips or knees but from a low board it will be found necessary to bend at the hips.' As multiple somersault dives came into being it became necessary to ball (tuck) the body up to complete the necessary rotation and so the tuck and pike positions eventually became recognized positions in addition to the straight position.

In the 1920 Olympics at Antwerp, the diving list included the Header Forward (Straight), the Hunch Dive (Tuck position) and Pike Dive as three *separate* dives. It was later decided to make them *one* dive, i.e. 'Forward Dive' to be performed in any one of the three positions at the choice of the diver. This applies now to all dives in each group.

Contest Revisions Over the years, diving contest conditions have undergone constant revision and been altered in the light of experience. In the period before 1924 the diving tables were very complex. There were six methods of executing each Forward or Reverse Dive. The take-off could be standing, or a running take-off from one foot, or a running take-off from both feet, and in each case a head-first entry could be made 'with or without hands' (in the latter case the arms held by the sides!). The competition itself consisted of ten compulsory dives and two 'post' dives. The 'post' dives were drawn by number out of a hat, and as they consisted of some of the most difficult dives on the list, it was an unnerving experience for a diver waiting for his 'post' dive to be drawn.

The 1928 Olympic diving competitions consisted of compulsory dives and voluntary dives. The compulsory dives were selected after each Olympic Games and were in force for the following four years.

This form of competition continued until the 1948 Games in London. From 1949 to 1956 all dives were voluntary dives on both spring and highboard, and very rarely were the *basic* dives ever seen in competition. After 1956, the regulations were revised again to include five required basic dives from the springboard. This brought a 'new look' to diving and did a great deal to ensure that divers mastered their basic dives before being encouraged to attempt the more difficult dives.

Early High Diving Platforms The platforms used by early divers were often temporary wooden scaffolding structures, far from rigid and erected outdoors, making diving from them in windy weather a perilous pursuit. The ascent to the 10 metre platform was usually by means of a vertical ladder which in itself was a hazardous procedure. For many years all 10 metre diving stages were constructed outdoors. For countries with warm weather for most of the year this presented no problems. A covered 10 metre diving stage is a costly project and for many years was considered an unnecessary luxury. As new building techniques and materials became available, it became a practical possibility. Indoor 10 metre diving facilities are now found in most countries allowing high-board training to take place all the year round instead of during just a few weeks in the summer season. In the Americas and Australasia the

10 metre platform is referred to as 'the Tower'.

The Olympic Games diving events were all held outdoors until 1948 when they were for the first time held indoors at the Wembley Empire Pool, London. Many modern diving stages incorporate a lift to take divers from the bathside to either the $7\frac{1}{2}$ metre platform or in some instances to the 10 metre stage, thus eliminating the exhausting climb prior to each dive.

Early High Diving in England From 1895 until 1922 the only opportunity to dive from 10 metres in England was for a brief period each summer at Highgate Pond when a temporary stage was erected on top of the existing 15 foot (4.6 m) platform. The authorities would sometimes leave the stage in position for a few weeks and so give divers their only opportunity for 10 metre practice. The L.C.C. erected a permanent concrete 10 metre structure in 1923 and for many years it became the diver's mecca.

The opening of the Empire Pool at Wembley in 1934 for the Empire Games, with its 10 metre stage, Olympic springboards, and 16 feet (4.88 m) of water, heralded a new era in diving history. The Olympic diving trials were held there in 1936, and the European Games in 1938. During the war it was closed, but it was reopened especially for the 1948 Olympic Games. Diving suffered a severe blow when it was decided to close the pool after the Games and to convert it into an ice rink and sports arena.

The Evolution of the Springboard The Paris Olympic Games in 1924 were notable for the introduction of the first standard International Springboard with a movable fulcrum brought over from the U.S.A. The American men and women divers made a clean sweep of all six Springboard medals. On these boards they produced a standard of execution that put them in a class way above any other country. In 1928 an American diver, Pete Desjardins, won both the High and Springboard diving events at the Amsterdam Games. He demonstrated dives never seen before from the springboard such as the Forward $1\frac{1}{2}$ Somersault with a Full Twist. He was invited to England in 1931 and again in 1934, 1935, 1936 and 1937 when his exhibitions inspired the divers of that period.

The early springboards were crude affairs compared with the highly scientific metal alloy board used today. The original 'spring boards' were simply planks of wood fixed together by cross battens with very little spring in them. Each country had its own design of springboards and visiting divers had to spend a considerable time getting used to the boards. The modern metal alloy board manufactured in the U.S.A. is so far in advance of any other board that its use has become general all over the world. This standardization of springboards has had a tremendous influence on the progress of international diving. England's first springboard was installed at Highgate Pond by the L.C.C. in 1923.

The Fulcrum Evolves In 1921 the Amateur Diving Association (England) stated that the 'outer point of support' for springboards should be placed 4 feet 6 inches (1.40 m) from the front end of the board. The early fulcrums were little more than wooden trestles fixed permanently to the deck. The 'springboards' were often bolted or strapped to the fulcrum, a practice which resulted in early breakage of the board due to a concentration of stresses at one point. All springboards now rest free on the fulcrum. Movable fulcrums were introduced in the early 'twenties which allowed the fulcrum to be adjusted by the diver, as a different fulcrum position is required for standing dives to that required for running dives. The modern freely adjustable fulcrum unit is a precision instrument made of steel which allows the diver to adjust the fulcrum roller easily at will. For the modern springboard 4.60 metres (16 ft) long, the fulcrum roller is set, when centred, at a point 3 metres (9 ft 10 in) from the front end. The first movable fulcrum unit to be used in the Olympic Games was brought over by the U.S.A. team for the Paris Games in 1924.

Women's Diving Regulations Women were allowed in the Olympic diving events for the first time at the Olympic Games in Stockholm in 1912, in a Plain Diving contest. Diving was considered unsuitable for women at that time and it was not until after the war in 1920 at the Olympic Games in Antwerp that women were allowed to compete in springboard events. Women were allowed to compete in a Highboard (Fancy) Diving event for the first time at the Amsterdam Olympics in 1928 (the men's and women's Plain Diving events having been discontinued after the 1924 Games). It was decided however that certain dives were not to be performed by women at all, and some other dives were to be performed by women from the 5 metre platform only. Their restriction lasted until the 1956 Olympic Games at Melbourne. In 1957 it was removed and from then on women could perform any dive listed in the tables.

U.S.A. Domination The First World War brought diving to a halt in Europe and the U.S.A. divers forged ahead to such an extent that when the Olympic Games restarted after the war in 1920 at Antwerp, they swept the board, gaining all six Springboard medals in the men's and women's events. This started the U.S.A. domination of the Olympic diving events. After the Second World War had ended in 1945, diving was in the doldrums in Europe. In 1948 England acted as host for the

first post-war Olympic Games. The diving events were held at the
Empire Pool Wembley and we again saw how supreme the U.S.A.
divers were. Mrs. Victoria Draves, U.S.A., won both Springboard and
High Diving events demonstrating a grace and excellence not seen
before. But it was Sammy Lee, the U.S.A. diver from California, who
captured the imagination of the spectators when he won the men's High
Diving. He went on to repeat his success in 1952 in Helsinki. His ease of
performance in such dives as the Forward $3\frac{1}{2}$ Somersault from the 10
metre board was unbelievable. 'Fancy' diving had come a long way in a
few years.

The U.S.A. men won every men's Springboard event from 1920 to
1968 and took every second place until 1968 when Dibiasi (Italy) came
second. Of the eleven Platform golds, the U.S.A. men won nine, being
beaten by Mexico (Capilla) in 1956 and Italy (Dibiasi) in 1968. The
U.S.A. women won every Springboard medal (coming first, second and
third) in the period 1920 to 1948. Mrs. June McComick, U.S.A., won
the Olympic Springboard and High Diving events in both 1952 and
1956, a remarkable feat. The U.S.A. women's run of golds was broken
by Ingrid Kramer (East Germany) who won both the Springboard and
High Diving golds in 1960 at Rome and the Springboard gold in 1964 at
Tokyo.

European Emergence   The Munich Olympics in 1972 saw a further
decline in U.S.A. domination. In the men's Springboard event Russia
came first, with Italy second and the U.S.A. third. In the men's Highboard Klaus Dibiasi (Italy) repeated his 1968 success and came first
with the U.S.A. in second place.

In the women's events, Micky King won the only diving gold for the
U.S.A. team, coming first in the Springboard final. In second place was
Ulrika Knape (Sweden) who went on to win the women's Highboard
event.

The largest threat for the future is in the Russian and East German
divers who have progressed to a very high standard and are obviously
out to break the already crumbling U.S.A. domination in world diving.
The indifferent climate in Northern Europe retarded progress in
diving there, but as more indoor diving facilities are provided, the gap
between the U.S.A. and the rest of the world is gradually being reduced.

The Commonwealth Games   The British Empire Games (now the
British Commonwealth Games) were first held at Hamilton (Canada) in
1903 with eleven competing countries. Called 'the friendly games' and
staged every four years in the same year as the European Games they
provided yet another encouragement to England who could not break
the power of the U.S.A. and Germany in world diving events.

Until 1966 England had won half the available Commonwealth gold medals. Brian Phelps (England) emerged as the most successful diver, becoming Springboard and Highboard champion in 1962 at Perth, Australia, and repeating his success in 1966 at Kingston, Jamaica. In 1966 England won all four events – men's and women's Springboard and Highboard. Peter Heatly (Scotland) won the gold Springboard in 1954 and gold Highboard in 1950 and 1958.

Then and Now In the early days of diving it was often a case of 'survival of the fittest'. Only those with courage combined with a high degree of gymnastic ability attempted it. For many years there were no textbooks to help understand the complexities of the sport. Training was a case of trial and error on the 'hit or miss' principle, with the diver getting more smacks than was comfortable. In recent years a more scientific approach to diving has been achieved, there have been great improvements in both conditions and facilities since the early beginnings of diving. This has resulted in a remarkable advance in the standard of performance of established dives and an increase in the complexity of new dives. In fifty years the sport has grown out of all recognition. Today youngsters are performing dives that would not have been considered possible fifty years ago even by experienced adults.

2. Diving Knowledge

Competitive diving is a firmly established sport internationally and is practised to a high degree of proficiency in all five continents. It has evolved from very small beginnings at the turn of the century to a highly skilled technical pursuit calling for considerable courage. During a contest, a diver has not only once but ten to eleven times to project himself high into the air from either a flexible springboard or from a high platform and perform many complex somersaulting and twisting dives in addition to the basic dives. From the high platform he plummets into the water head first at over 30 m.p.h. (48 km.p.h.).

Unfortunately the word 'diving' does little to convey this sort of picture to the man in the street. It is often used to describe any method of descending beneath the surface of the water. We speak of a submarine diving, a deep sea diver in his rubber suit and steel helmet, and of pearl divers. In life-saving the 'surface dive' is used to descend quickly from the surface to the bottom. In underwater swimming there is 'skin diving' using the snorkel, and 'aqualung diving' using the compressed air container. Swimmers use the 'racing dive' to enter the water from the side of the pool. In all these instances the dive is used as a means to an end, the aim being to descend deep or in the case of the racing dive to project the body as far forward as possible beneath the surface.

Competitive Diving In competitive diving, however, the water is just the landing medium as the mat is for the gymnast. It is the flight through the air that is the dive and provides the challenge. Basically the sport of diving as practised today requires taking off from a height, and aiming to remain free in the air for as long as possible. During the flight the body may be held in various positions at the choice of the diver whilst he performs either a graceful header or a more complicated dive consisting of a variety of somersaulting and/or twisting movements before entering the water.

Diving enables you to do something that can be achieved in few other sports, that is to fly through the air without any means of support and land safely without discomfort. It enables the average person to perform many gymnastic feats that he would find difficult if not impossible to do in a gymnasium. Whereas the gymnast must always finish his movement with a feet-first landing, the diver has the choice of finishing feet first or head first. Unlike the gymnast landing on the firm floor and able to control his balance within fairly wide limits, the diver has little or no control of his position as he enters the water. If he overthrows on entry there is little he can do about it.

The more *time* a diver has in the air the easier it is for him to finish the dive with a controlled entry. To remain in the air for as long as possible the diver requires height. This height is obtained either by diving from a high platform or projecting oneself high into the air from a springboard.

Platform Diving   The platform is a rigid fixture covered with a resilient hardwood surface from which the diver takes off. The hardwood surface must be covered throughout with coconut matting or provided with a satisfactory non-slip surface matting. It is installed at heights of 5 metres and 10 metres above the water level, with additional training platforms at heights of 1 metre, 3 metres and 7½ metres where possible. The regulations require that the 10 metre platform be 2 metres wide and 6 metres long with the front end projecting at least 1.5 metres beyond the edge of the bath. The staging on which the platforms are mounted may be of any suitable rigid construction, usually reinforced concrete or steel. Mechanical surface agitation should be installed under the diving facilities to aid divers in their visual perception of the surface of the water.

Springboard Diving   The modern springboard is a flexible, tapered, precision instrument from which the diver springs upwards to obtain extra height in his dive, giving him more time in the air. An expert can rise 5 feet (1.50 m) above the board. Springboards are installed at heights of 1 metre and 3 metres above the water level. The regulations require that the springboards be at least 4.8 metres long and 0.5 metres wide and covered along the whole length with rough coconut-matting unless provided with a satisfactory non-slip surface. The springboards must be provided with movable fulcrums easily adjustable by the diver, and should be installed dead level with the front end, projecting at least 1.5 metres beyond the edge of the bath. The modern wooden springboard consists of selected timber strips glued together then tapered on the underside towards both ends in a parabolic curve and totally encased in glass fibre. This has been superseded in international competition by the all-metal board made from an aluminium alloy combining tremendous springing properties with lightness.

Regulations   Diving is an enjoyable and satisfying sport, providing a challenge to the spirit of daring present in every boy and girl. Although one may never feel the desire to compete, the basic rules and requirements of competitive diving can be studied with advantage as they provide a ready guide and yardstick by which progress may be measured.

The diving regulations have evolved after many years of trial and error and are the result of experience gained by many highly skilled performers. A certain amount of desirable standardization has been reached in the execution of the various dives, providing a ready-made structure on which to base one's training.

Dives   There are approximately seventy different dives listed. Each dive has a different *number* and may be performed in one of three recognized *body positions*. The dives are divided into six *groups*.

Dives are created by divers themselves and if approved are included in the tariff tables. In the early days dives were often named after their originators. Two Swedish divers, Isander (Reverse Dive) and Molberg (Reverse Somersault) gave their names in this way.

A dive begins the moment the *starting position* is assumed and consists of the *take-off* from the board, the *flight* through the air and the *entry* into the water. The dive is finished the moment the body is completely submerged. All front-facing dives may be performed either from a standing or from a running take-off. All dives are some form of somersault, the basic header is a half Somersault. This is followed by the Single Somersault, $1\frac{1}{2}$ Somersault, Double Somersault, $2\frac{1}{2}$ Somersault, Triple Somersault and finally the $3\frac{1}{2}$ Somersault. The direction of the rotation can be either forward or backward. The $\frac{1}{2}$, $1\frac{1}{2}$, $2\frac{1}{2}$ and $3\frac{1}{2}$ Somersault Dives are head-first entries, but the Single, Double and Triple Somersaults enter feet first. As feet-first entries are more difficult to control, the majority of divers select head-first entries in competition. The diver takes off from the board either facing the water or with his back to the water. The combining of each direction of rotation with both types of take-off produce four basic groups of dives, Forward, Back, Reverse and Inward.

The Groups   A system of division was instituted in 1929 in which dives are grouped according to the starting position on the board (facing front or with the back to the water) and the direction of rotation during the flight through the air (either forward or backward) as follows:

Table A   SPRINGBOARD DIVING

Group 1.   Forward Dives – front start with forward rotation
Group 2.   Back Dives – back start with backward rotation
Group 3.   Reverse Dives – front start with backward rotation
Group 4.   Inward Dives – back start with forward rotation
Group 5.   Twist Dives – rotation about the body's long axis in
             addition to the forward or backward rotation from
             either a front or back starting position

Plate 2. Klaus Dibiasi *(Italy) World Highboard Champion 1973 (Belgrade):*
Armstand Position

Table B PLATFORM DIVING
Groups 1 to 5 as in Table A Springboard Diving, plus:
Group 6.   Armstand Dives – any dive commencing from an arm-
stand position

Prior to 1953, Group 4 Inward Dives were called 'Backward Spring Forward Dives'. In the early days of diving, Reverse Dives were known as 'Gainers', Inward Dives as 'Cutaway Dives', and Twist Dives as 'Screw Dives' and 'Borers'. No Twist Dives were performed from high-boards prior to the 1948 Olympics. The Twist group is the largest as it consists of Forward Back, Reverse and Inward dives with twist. The amount of twist varies between a half twist up to three twists.

The Numbering System   The present system of identification was introduced after the 1956 Olympic Games in Melbourne. Prior to this, dives were only numbered consecutively from 1 to 56. As international diving contests became more numerous it became increasingly necessary to overcome the language difficulty and find some method of ensuring that divers and judges were absolutely sure of the dive to be performed.

Each dive in the four basic groups is given a three-figure number. The first figure reading from the left denotes the group, 1 (Forward), 2 (Back), 3 (Reverse) or 4 (Inward). The second figure shows whether or not a flying movement is incorporated (a flying movement is indicated by 1, a non-flying movement by 0) and the third figure indicates the amount of rotation required (in increments of a half somersault). Dives can now be quickly and easily identified by numbers, irrespective of the language of the country of origin.

In each group, dives rise in difficulty by increments of a half somer-sault. The basic dive (header) in each group being one half somersault and given the number 1 (the third digit from the left). A complete somer-sault would be numbered 2; a $1\frac{1}{2}$ somersault 3; and so on. Dive No. 101 (a) would be a Forward Dive in the straight position: the first digit indicating Group 1 (Forward); the second, no flying movement; the third, one half somersault (a header), and (a) indicating 'straight', (the manner of execution or body position). The Forward Dive can also be executed in the pike position as No. 101 (b) or in the tuck position as No. 101(c). Most dives may be performed in each of the three recognized body positions but as they have the same number they are considered the same dive, the choice of position being left to the diver. The follow-ing examples will make the system clear:

Dive No. 105c	Forward $2\frac{1}{2}$ Somersault Tuck
Dive No. 203b	Back $1\frac{1}{2}$ Somersault Pike
Dive No. 312c	Reverse Flying Somersault Tuck
Dive No. 401a	Inward Dive Straight

In the Twist group, a four-figure coding system is used. The first figure '5' denotes Twist Group, the second figure denotes the basic group number, the third figure indicates the number of half somersaults, and the fourth figure the number of half lateral turns (Twist) e.g. Dive No. 5132 would be translated as Twist Group, Forward Group, $1\frac{1}{2}$ Somersaults, 1 Twist, and announced as 'Forward $1\frac{1}{2}$ Somersault 1 Twist'.

In the Armstand group a three-figure code is used as follows: the first figure denotes the group (Armstand), the second figure denotes the direction of rotation, i.e. forward – 1 or backward – 2, and the third figure, the amount of rotation in increments of a half somersault. The numbering system enables everyone, divers, officials and spectators of any country present quickly and easily to identify by sight the dive to be performed even before it has been announced.

The Flight The flight is that part of the dive when the body is free in the air. The flight commences the moment the feet (the hands in Armstand Dives) leave the board at the completion of the take-off, and is finished the moment any part of the body touches the water for the entry. During the flight through the air the body may be carried in one of three recognized body positions. The only exception occurs with a number of somersault dives with twist, when the position is 'free'.

During the flight through the air the diver is able to control his rate of rotation (angular velocity) within certain limits. The tighter he tucks, the faster he spins; the more he opens out, the slower he spins. When he stretches out ready for his entry he will be rotating at his slowest, but he cannot stop the rotation entirely so must make allowance for this to achieve the desired vertical entry.

The beauty of the dive depends a great deal on body and limb alignment during the flight. The arm position is at the choice of the diver and influences to a great extent the look of the dive. During the flight the feet must be together with the toes pointed. A diver's physique may enhance or spoil the execution of the dive during the flight. The shape of the leg, especially at the knee, and the ability to point the toes have a great bearing on the general assessment of the dive in the eyes of both spectator and judge.

Body Positions During the passage through the air the body can be carried *straight*, with *pike* or with *tuck*.
(a) Straight – The body shall not be bent either at the knees or at the hips, the feet shall be together and the toes pointed.
(b) Pike – The body shall be bent at the hips, but the legs must be kept straight at the knees, with toes pointed.

(c) Tuck – The whole body is bunched up with the knees together, hands on the lower legs and toes pointed.

The position of the arms in each case is at the choice of the diver. In the case of the Straight and the Pike positions, there are accepted variations which although different, still comply with the regulations (Fig. 1).

Fig. 1. The Body Positions

Variations of Position All Forward and Inward Dives in the Straight position are usually performed with the back held straight, while Back and Reverse Dives in the Straight position are executed with the back arched.

There are three accepted Pike positions. The 'dive' in which the hands touch the feet, the 'open' with the hips bent at 90° and the arms extended sideways, and the 'close' position with the hands behind the legs pulling the shoulders to the knees.

The 'dive' position is used for the basic dives in the Pike position in the Forward, Back, Reverse and Inward groups. The hands are usually placed on the instep as near the toes as possible with the arms held straight.

For slow rotating dives, such as the Forward $1\frac{1}{2}$ Somersault from the 10 metre platform, the open Pike position would normally be used.

Plate 3. Klaus Dibiasi *(Italy) World Highboard Champion 1973 (Belgrade)* ; *Olympic Highboard Champion 1968 (Mexico) and 1972 (Munich) : Forward* $1\frac{1}{2}$ *Somersault Pike*

For fast rotation, as required for a Forward $3\frac{1}{2}$ Somersault, the close Pike position with the arms bent at the elbows with the hands behind the legs pulling the shoulders to the knees is usually adopted.

The body positions are assumed soon after take-off and held for varying lengths of time during the flight depending on the requirements of the dive being performed. For example, during a $3\frac{1}{2}$ Tuck Somersault from a 10 metre board the Tuck position would be held for the major part of the dive until just prior to entry, but in a simple Tuck Somersault from the 10 metre board the Tuck position would only be shown for a very brief period at the beginning, the remainder of the dive being performed in the Straight position with the hands above the head.

Free Position   In competition, the diver selects the most suitable body position for the dive being performed, (a), (b) or (c). Most dives in the four basic groups may be executed in at least two positions, some in all three. In the majority of somersaulting dives in the Twist group it is not possible to assume a set position throughout. During the actual twisting movement the body is held practically straight, and when the required number of twists have been completed the body usually assumes a Pike position to complete the required amount of rotation. To overcome this problem the 'free position' was created after the Rome Olympics in 1960 and given the designation (d).

Choice of Position   The choice of body position for a particular dive depends on the diver's physique, and the difficulty of the dive in relation to his ability. The body rotates (somersaults) slowest when straight, twice as fast in the Pike position and four times as fast in the Tuck position. The degree of difficulty allocated to a dive executed in the Straight position is therefore usually greater than for the same dive performed piked. The 'Tuck' usually has the lowest degree of difficulty as it enables the body to rotate at its fastest and therefore complete a given number of revolutions in less time. When the body is straightened out for entry from a Tuck position, its rate of rotation will be reduced considerably giving the diver greater control over the entry. This control at entry is available to a lesser extent with the body rotating in the 'Pike' and hardly at all to a body rotating in the straight position.

The Starting Position   This is a required position, generally referred to as the 'stance', taken up by the diver before commencing the take-off. The starting position for *standing* dives is assumed when the competitor stands on the front end of the springboard or platform either facing the water (front stance) or back to the water (back stance). The body should be straight, head erect, with the arms straight by the sides or above the head.

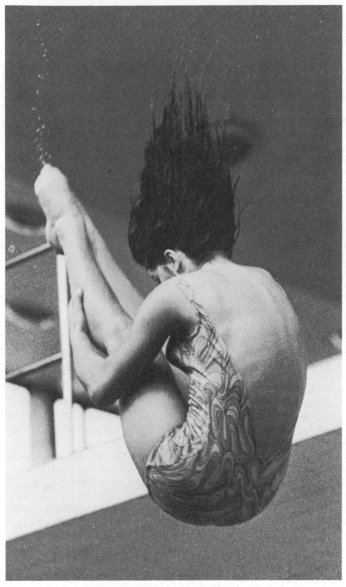

Plate 4. Christine Lindener *(West Germany): Inward* $1\frac{1}{2}$ *Somersault Pike*

The starting position for *running* dives is assumed when the diver is ready to take the first step of the run. In competitive diving there must be a minimum of four steps including the take-off. This requires taking up the front stance at least four paces back from the front end of the springboard or platform.

The starting position for *armstand* dives is assumed when the diver has placed both hands on the front end of the platform ready to throw or press up into a balance. The starting positions are defined so exactly because the judging of the dive commences directly the starting position is assumed.

The Front Stance *(Facing the Water)*   This is the starting position used for Forward and Reverse dives performed from a standing take-off. The feet may be together with heels touching or apart to assist balance. The toes may be on the board or curled over the edge at the choice of the diver.

The Back Stance *(Back to the Water)*   This is the starting position used for Back and Inward dives. The feet may be together with heels touching or apart to assist balance. The body weight should be distributed evenly on the balls of the feet with the heels projecting beyond the end of the board. To take up the position, the diver should walk to the front end of the board and turn round so that the heels are about 3 inches (80 mm) from the end. One foot is then moved back into position followed by the other. The back stance is a much less stable position than the front stance because the heels are clear of the board making it a more difficult position to maintain.

The Take-off   For a standing dive, the take-off starts from the commencement of the armswing, and for a running dive, from the commencement of the run, and is completed the moment the feet leave the board. From the springboard, the 'run' is performed at a walking pace and the take-off from the end of the board must be *from both feet simultaneously*. From the firmboard it is a definite run, but the actual take-off from the end of the board can be from one or both feet. In both cases the run should be smooth, straight and without hesitation. There must be continual forward progression. The take-off should be from the end of the board and should be bold, reasonably high and confident. The take-off is the most important part of the dive. What is seen during the flight is the result of what took place at the take-off. The correct execution of all dives depends more on the take-off than any other factor. Errors at take-off cannot be corrected during the flight. The take-off requires perfect co-ordination of the movements of the body and limbs. From the springboard these body movements must also be co-ordinated with the movement of the board. Before the diver loses contact with the board at the completion of the take-off, three objects must be achieved:

(1) The body must be set in motion *away from the board* for safety.
(2) The body must be projected *upwards* with maximum velocity to obtain *height* with its resultant gain in *time*.
(3) The body movements necessary to produce the forward or backward *rotation* must be completed.

After the diver has lost contact with the board the die is cast, there is little he can do to alter his dive.

The Entry   The entry is the final part of the dive at the end of the flight, commencing the moment any part of the body touches the water and finishing when the body is completely submerged. The regulations require that: 'The entry into the water must in all cases be vertical or nearly so, with the body straight, toes pointed. All head-first entries shall be executed with the arms stretched beyond the head in line with the body, with the hands close together, all feet-first entries with the arms close to the body and no bending at the elbows.' In the head-first entry it is important to note that the *top* of the head should make contact with the water and not the forehead. The limbs and body should then pass through the 'hole' in the water made by the hands. Subject to the requirements of the entry technique being employed, the body should be held firm and straight until the toes have disappeared beneath the surface.

The final assessment of a dive will be influenced to a considerable extent by the perfection or otherwise of the entry. The desired vertical entry requires adequate depth of water. A vertical entry from a fast rotating dive such as a Forward 3½ Somersault is very difficult to achieve as the rotation cannot be stopped, only slowed down, so the diver aims to enter the water a little short of vertical to avoid going past the vertical. An entry past the vertical is usually beyond control. Various 'saving' techniques have been developed in which the diver bends or arches beneath the surface to prevent the legs going over, after the trunk has entered the water. It is easier to effect a vertical entry from a 'head-first' dive than a 'feet-first' one. For this reason feet-first entries are never seen in modern contests. The dive is considered to be finished when the whole body is completely beneath the surface of the water.

The International Tariff   This is a points value system in the form of a number allocated to each dive increasing in value with the increase in difficulty of the dive. The judges' award for each dive is multiplied by the degree-of-difficulty tariff value attached to it to arrive at the final score for that dive. (Judges do not take the difficulty of the dive into account when giving their awards.) As an example, the simplest dive in tariff tables is the Forward Dive Tuck, rated at 1.2 from the 1 metre springboard, whereas the Forward $3\frac{1}{2}$ Somersault Pike from the 3 metre springboard is rated 3.0. The degree-of-difficulty tariff tables are drawn up by the FINA International Diving Committee and are reviewed every four years immediately after the Olympic Games. Tariff tables were drawn up and used in the Olympic Games for the first time in London (White City) in 1908.

It would be a simple matter of comparison if each diver in a competition performed the same dive. Each judge would award points on the standard of execution seen. An example of this is a school competition in which the Plain Header is performed by all competitors. In some school competitions the divers are allowed to perform a *voluntary* dive in addition to the set dives. The more timid diver will probably elect to do another simple Header but one or two may decide to attempt more difficult dives such as a Back Dive or Somersault. As a judge, you have to decide whether a simple Header done well from the side is worth more or less than a Somersault performed only moderately well from the top board. It is a difficult task to be fair in such circumstances and could never be allowed in an important competition.

The degree of difficulty takes into account the position of the dive (a), (b) or (c), the height of the board it is performed from, and the type of board. The judge has only to award points for the execution of the dive. The difficulty of the dive is covered by the tariff value.

Apart from facilitating judging and the running of competitions generally, the tariff tables provide a ready-made list of progressions for a diver's training. You are also able to decide whether a particular dive is worth doing. You may have to choose between a simple dive with a low tariff, which you know you can do well, or a more difficult dive with a high tariff, which you cannot perform well consistently. The same applies to the *position* of the dive. The Forward Dive from the 1 metre springboard has a different tariff value for each of its three positions. You have to consider whether to perform it in the low tariff Tuck position (1.2) with its ease of performance, or the higher value Straight position (1.4) with the difficulty of achieving a controlled vertical entry, or the Pike position (1.3) with its ease of control. As a general rule it is wiser to choose a dive that you know you can do well rather than go 'chasing tariff'.

Requirements Although diving has the same governing body as swimming, there is no real connection between the two sports other than that a diver must be able to swim to get out of the pool. The two sports usually attract a different type of person. Swimming requires stamina and endurance qualities with little skill, whereas diving requires skill, courage and nerve. As with all skills, once learnt, little training is needed to keep the skill at a high level of performance. Training consists in building up one skill upon another, progressing gradually from the simpler movements to the more complex. Although there have been self-taught divers, it is generally recognized that to become successful a diver needs a coach. Divers sometimes train under far from ideal conditions. When performing back dives from the highboards, the diver has his back to the water and cannot see if anyone is in his way in the pool below him. He relies implicitly on his coach, when the coach says 'right' he dives. Competitive diving is not a dangerous sport, any accidents that happen today are usually caused through faulty techniques. In the past, accidents were due more often to poor or badly installed equipment. Springboards with too great a rise from back to front, and boards with loose or badly worn coconut matting were the worst offenders. Injuries through hitting the bottom are unknown if pools complying with FINA regulations are used. This type of injury is by far the most dangerous, but it only occurs in older-type pools where the depth of water beneath the boards does not comply with modern requirements.

Equipment The only personal equipment the male diver needs is a well-fitting pair of trunks. The normal elastic cord in many trunks is not sufficient to keep them in place when diving from a height. An internal nylon tying cord is essential under these conditions. External belts are useless as they cannot stand the impact with the water on entry.

Girls need a well-fitting, one-piece costume with strong shoulder straps. It is often worth while reinforcing the existing shoulder straps at the point where they join the costume.

The rest of the equipment is supplied by your local authority so diving is not an expensive sport. The question of caps may be left to the individual, although some authorities insist on caps for girls and women. Most divers either keep their hair cut short or ensure that it is securely tied at the back. Some continental countries insist on *all* bathers wearing caps so it is as well to take one with you when travelling abroad. Nose clips are sometimes worn by divers with nasal disorders, but this is usually troublesome on feet-first entries only. Ear plugs should not be used unless specified by a doctor. Needless to say, any form of activity which requires deep submergence in water should be avoided if you are suffering from any form of ear, nose or throat infection.

3. Safety

The early diving stages were erected over whatever water happened to be available. It was mostly outdoors, often cold and murky and the divers of the period had to be a hardy breed. To quote from an article published about 1910: 'When diving, care must be taken that the water is clear of piles or posts or large stones; it has very often happened that a diver in an unfamilar spot has hurt his head against old posts, which did not reach the surface of the water. Further, it must be a rule always by suitable movements to rise quickly to the surface. There must always be deep water, at least 10 ft. [3 m] at the spot where diving exercises are carried out.'

The article goes on to say: 'If a diver enters backwards he may become bewildered and swim downwards instead of upwards. If you remain quiet, you will drift upwards, so know the direction to the surface.' It may seem difficult for a young diver today, used to the crystal clear water of the modern pool, to appreciate these conditions. Anyone, however, who has had the unpleasant experience of descending into dark murky water will know only too well how disconcerting and dangerous it can be. Nearly everyone has the opportunity today to dive at an indoor pool, without the dangers present when diving in open waters.

The questions often asked are: 'What then are the dangers in diving; what sort of injuries can be caused, and how can they be avoided?' Injuries may be caused through (1) landing flat, (2) bad entries, (3) striking the board, (4) pressure on the ears and (5) hitting the bottom.

Landing Flat   Injuries caused through hitting the water awkwardly are seldom serious. If one lands flat, it stings for a moment but soon passes. Later there may be some bruising. When landing on the back, a pain will be felt in the chest, and if the landing is on the front, the pain will be felt in the back. The attachments of the inner organs etc. to the rib cage and spine are put under severe strain when the body hits the water. The inner organs continue downwards, pulling on their attachments.

Bad Entries   Lower back injuries are common with beginners. This occurs if the legs are allowed to overthrow on forward rotating entries, or if the diver arches up too soon i.e., before the body is completely submerged. Girls suffer most in this respect as they are more supple in the back and less strong in the abdominal region than boys.

When a beginner goes over on a forward entry with the back arched, as is usually the case, a severe jar may be given to the lumbar spine. On entry, the water holds the upper part of the body allowing the legs to go over. A diver should be taught to contract his abdomen during the flight and maintain a slight bend at the hips as he enters the water. In this way the abdominal muscles take the strain and not the spinal column. The golden rule is, never progress to a higher board if there is any tendency towards going over on entry. Arching up too soon on entry is a natural fear reaction. The beginner must be encouraged to go deeper before arching up to the surface.

Striking the Board   Injuries through striking the board are generally confined to the head. These occur mainly with dives from the Inward and Reverse groups and are mostly caused through a faulty take-off. The most serious injuries occur with such dives as the Inward and Reverse $2\frac{1}{2}$ Somersaults from the springboard and although severe at times, rarely cause injuries of a permanent nature. Any injury to the head should, however, be taken seriously and medical advice sought.

Ear Trouble   Anyone suffering from catarrh or any form of ear trouble or even a head cold should NEVER descend deeper than about 10 feet (3 m). Infection of the inner ear may occur under these conditions or worse still, a perforated ear drum. Water pressure increases with depth at the rate of $\frac{1}{2}$lb/sq in (0.03 kg/sq cm) for every foot (0.30 m) of the descent. It is very important to 'clear the ears' i.e., grip the nose, close the mouth and blow, when you reach deep water. Your ears should 'pop'. If you cannot clear them, do not go deep.

Hitting the Bottom   The greatest danger in diving is hitting the bottom with the head. This has, in some instances, caused partial paralysis through injury to the spinal cord, and in extreme cases death. This rarely affects the competitive diver because the depths he uses are normally governed by the official regulations. It is the self-taught diver who is most prone to this sort of accident. The beginner usually arches up on entry through natural fear, and so rarely descends deep. When the self-taught diver has overcome his fear, he will tend to descend deeper and may not be aware that his hands are not in front of his head, in a protective position. He may not realize that he should open his eyes under water to see how near he is to the bottom. He is in danger, because he is unaware of danger. The seriousness of any injury caused through striking the head on the bottom is increased as the entry approaches the vertical.

Extent of Injury   The location of injury is usually the cervical (neck) part of the spine. There may be a fracture or dislocation of the verte-brae. This in itself is not serious, but it is often accompanied by injury to the spinal cord which may result in paralysis of the upper part of the body including the limbs. Those responsible for applying first aid in such cases must prevent further injury by wrong handling of the head. When the head is submerged it is supported by the water. Support to the head must be given during the rescue operation making sure that it is not allowed to move from its normal position. The best first aid appli-ance is a special stretcher with head support placed in the water behind the patient. The patient is strapped to the stretcher whilst in the water. This prevents movement of the head which may cause further damage to the spinal cord.

Protecting the Head To protect the head from contact with the bottom, the arms must be held extended beyond the head until most of the body's momentum has been absorbed. This will occur soon after the body becomes completely submerged. Although children may show this arm position on entry, many of them will break immediately under the surface. Their arms will usually be forced sideways to a position by the body, leaving the head unprotected. This essential protective arm position should be taught from the beginning so that it becomes an automatic action at the completion of every dive.

Early Indoor Diving When indoor pools became available (the first was built in 1828 at Liverpool) they were built for swimming. The maximum depth at the deep end was never more than 6 feet (1.8 m). As diving became more popular, springboards and tiered diving stages were erected in some pools. The shallow water, however, made vertical entries impossible to attempt. The modern filtration plant was unknown and it was often not possible to see the bottom. To prevent hitting the bottom, divers would aim to enter at about 45° and would arch up on entry to avoid going too deep. Today the water is kept clear and hygienic and is heated to between 76°F (24°C) and 86°F (30°C) so that apart from the comfort, it is possible to see the bottom in 16 feet (4.88 m) of water easily.

The Vertical Entry As deeper pools have become available, a near vertical entry with the body stretched has become a practical possibility. This type of entry has a great influence on a judge's final assessment of a dive, so competitive divers practise to achieve this form of entry. This has resulted in the request for deeper and yet deeper water to avoid any possibility of hitting the bottom. Apart from its aesthetic appeal, the near vertical entry is the safest and most comfortable method of entering water *providing the water is deep enough*. If the water is not deep enough it is the most *dangerous* method of entering the water.

Safety Requirements What is a safe depth of water for diving? This question is often asked, but the answer is not quite as simple as it would at first appear to be. The requirements of a safe depth of water should allow for a near vertical entry with good form, i.e. with the body stretched straight. It should not require any special underwater saving technique such as arching the back, somersaulting or the use of shock-absorbing tactics with the arms. It should allow the diver to dive with complete confidence without fear of hitting the bottom.

The factors that determine a safe depth of water are not affected to any great extent by whether the dive performed is simple or advanced, or whether the diver is an expert or a beginner. The governing factors are purely mechanical and physical. The factors to be considered are the height and weight of the diver, and the distance he drops.

Diver's Height To avoid injury, no one should dive *vertically* (not even from the bathside) into water less deep than their fully stretched height, i.e. with the feet pointed and arms extended above the head. This, in the case of some older boys can be as much as 8 feet (2.50 m) and in the case of younger boys only 5 feet (1.50 m). As the body descends it is opposed by the upthrust of the water it displaces, but the full buoyancy effect does not come into operation until the body is *completely submerged*, therefore a tall diver needs greater depth than a short diver.

The Critical Depth Underwater observation of bathside dives shows that when the body is completely submerged, the downward velocity decreases rapidly. At a depth approaching 6 feet (1.90 m) the body is travelling fast, and the time taken for the head to reach this distance is very short (about $\frac{1}{4}$ second). At about 8 feet (2.50 m) the head is travelling much slower having taken about $\frac{3}{4}$ second to travel the remaining 2 feet (0.60 m). An adult diver entering vertically from the side into 6 feet (1.80 m) of water would find it difficult to stop by placing his hands on the bottom. The same dive into 8 feet (2.50 m) of water would present no problems. The critical depth is the one providing complete submergence, in which the body becomes weightless, leaving only the momentum at entry to be absorbed.

When entering vertically from the bathside, a depth of water equal to one's fully stretched height with arms extended above the head and feet pointed provides a reasonable margin of safety. When the feet are submerged the body is weightless and the head is the length of the lower arm from the bottom. In actual practice the diver will usually raise his head at this point and arch his back deflecting his body from the bottom. This action will also increase the resistance of the body and will cause a further rapid slowing down of its descent.

Entry Consideration   The time taken from the moment of entry until the feet are submerged is very short and there is a brief moment on entry when the eyes automatically close and the mind goes blank. Diving into water as deep as the extended body just allows time for the diver to become aware of his position and he will then usually lift his head and guide himself along the bottom quite safely. Any depth less than this requires very quick reflexes in the diver in order that he can employ instinctively some method of avoiding contact with the bottom, but he will only do this if he is *aware of danger*. This is why the first dive into a strange pool can be dangerous. A diver should always enter feet-first to test the depth and for his first head-first entry always enter from the lowest level possible.

Diver's Weight   This is the most important factor. Whereas children's height in general is related to age, weight may differ considerably in children of the same age group. For example, two boys of sixteen may weigh 8 stone (50 kg) and 12 stone (75 kg) respectively, although they may not differ much in height. On entering the water a diver's body possesses momentum as a product of its mass and its velocity at entry. Therefore the momentum is proportionate to the weight. This momentum must be 'absorbed' by the water. It follows that greater momentum will require greater depth of water to allow sufficient time for the greater momentum to be 'absorbed'. In other words, in a given depth of water a heavy boy will strike the bottom with much more force than a lighter boy.

Distance Fallen   From a given height, all divers, irrespective of their body weight, will enter the water at the same speed. The velocity at entry is dependant only on the distance fallen. As momentum is a product of mass and its velocity at entry, diving from a greater height will give increased velocity at entry and greater momentum to be 'absorbed' requiring greater depth. In actual practice it is found that after a depth of about $8\frac{1}{2}$ feet (2.60 m) the additional depth of water required is only a fraction of the additional drop from a higher board.

Adaptation to Depth   Over a period of time, a diver becomes conditioned to entering a particular depth of water. He gradually builds up a number of protective reflexes that enable him to continue in such a depth. His body *adapts* to the prevailing conditions. Many divers in the past learned their diving in only 6 feet of water without accident, and may find it difficult to believe that deeper water is needed today.

A diver who has learnt to dive into shallow water becomes *conditioned* to the depth and may continue to dive without injury. But when given the opportunity to dive into deep water, then he must be extremely careful when attempting to dive again into shallower water. It is under these circumstances that many of the injuries to divers occur. When a diver becomes conditioned to diving into deep water, it becomes very difficult to *consciously* act fast enough to avoid contact with the bottom in shallower water even though he may be aware of danger. Although a diver may be able to train himself to use shallow water he should not be expected to.

The Entry Angle The vertical entry provides the quickest way to the bottom. It is difficult to avoid a near vertical entry when diving from heights above 1 metre. From the bathside or 1 metre board it is quite easy to enter at any angle from near vertical to near horizontal. The diver's first duty is to check the depth before attempting to dive. If there is any suggestion of the water being too shallow for vertical entries then the angle at entry must be altered to suit the depth. Let us assume that for an adult entering *vertically* from the bathside we need a depth of 8 feet (2.44 m) to ensure that he is fully submerged before his hands touch the bottom.

The following chart (Fig. 2) shows what depth is required to allow him to be fully submerged at various angles of entry.

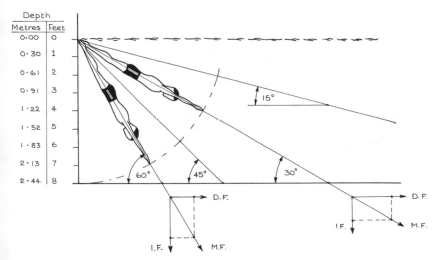

Fig. 2. An angled entry needs less depth. M.F. represents the maximum force, I.F. the impact force and D.F. the deflection force

Entry Angle and Depth An entry at an angle of 60° to the surface will need a depth of only 7 feet (2.13 m) to allow the diver to be fully submerged. Entering at 45° would need only 5 feet 7 inches (1.70 m), and entering at an angle of 30° would need only 4 feet (1.20 m), exactly half the depth required for a vertical entry. A shallow entry at 15° to the surface as for the normal 'plunge in to swim' type of entry would require a depth of only 2 feet (0.61 m) for the diver to become fully submerged.

Comparing the *distance* along the projected line of flight from the surface to the bottom at a given depth, we find the following. With a vertical depth of 8 feet (2.44 m) the distance travelled for a 60° entry is 9 feet 3 inches (2.82 m). For an entry at 45° the distance is 11 feet 6 inches (3.50 m). At 30° the distance is 16 feet (4.88 m), and for the 15° entry 31 feet (9.45 m).

Apart from its value in allowing for diving into shallower water, the angled entry has one other important advantage. The projected line of flight strikes the bottom at an angle, so it is much easier for the diver to deflect himself from the bottom by arching the back and lifting the head.

The Impact Force The force of impact, should the head strike the bottom, is at its maximum with the vertical entry. It gets less as the angle of entry is decreased. A parallelogram of forces drawn at the angle of entry shows this clearly (Fig. 2). M.F. represents the maximum force which is along the projected line of flight. D.F. represents the horizontal deflection force and I.F. the vertical impact force. To take an example, at 60° the impact force is greater than the deflection force, but at 30° the impact force is less than the deflection force. Let us assume that the maximum force is 10 units in both cases, then at 60° the impact force is 8¼ units and at 30° the impact force is only 5 units, i.e. half of the maximum force.

Safety Precautions I. The ideal vertical entry should only be attempted if the water is deep enough. When diving into water less deep than this, the entry should be angled to suit the depth.

II. The angle of entry should be such that the body is completely submerged before the outstretched hands touch the bottom, e.g. an entry at an angle of 45° into 6 feet (1.83 m) of water would allow for a distance of 8½ feet (2.60 m) between the point of entry and contact with the bottom.

III. Children should be taught to keep their arms extended beyond the head for protection whenever they enter the water head first.

IV. Always check the depth by jumping in feet first before attempting a head-first vertical entry.

In a bath that allows unsupervised diving by all members of the public, the facilities should cater for a tall, heavy adult entering vertically head first, therefore the competitive requirements of the A.S.A. should be complied with for safety purposes. **Under no circumstances should diving boards be used in pools with a deep end of only 6 feet 6 inches (1.98 m) deep.**

Supervised Diving   In a school bath when diving is done under supervision and by children who use the bath regularly, diving can be carried out safely in water shallower than that officially recommended for competition. This would also apply in a public bath used regularly by schoolchildren under supervision. We can say therefore that to provide a reasonable margin of safety for schoolchildren, no diving should be attempted from a 1 metre springboard or firmboards up to 6 feet (1.80 m) from the surface into water less than $8\frac{1}{2}$ feet deep (2.60 m). This depth allows the greater part of the body's momentum to be absorbed and although the diver may touch the bottom with outstretched hands his velocity will be reduced considerably. He will usually tuck up and push off from the bottom. The weight of older boys, who are often 6 feet (1.80 m) in height and may weigh up to 12 stone (76 kg), must be taken into account when diving under these conditions.

No diving should be allowed from 3 metre springboards or firmboards above 6 feet (1.80 m) and up to 16 feet (4.88 m) in height unless the water is at least 10 feet (3 m) deep. Every attempt should be made to hold *inter-school* contests at establishments with the required A.S.A. conditions regulating the depth of water, i.e.

9 ft 10 in (3 m) for 1 metre springboard
11 ft 6 in (3.50 m) for 3 metre springboard
12 ft 6 in (3.80 m) for 5 metre firmboard

These depths were fixed for baths built between 1953 and 1969. Baths built after 1969 are required to have greater depths than this.

4. *Teaching Diving*

Most swimmers have the urge to enter the water head first but not all are fortunate enough to receive instruction in how this is done. Many children learn to swim without learning to dive, although swimming instruction should include methods of entering the water in a variety of ways. The young swimmer should be able to enter feet first or head first, and be able to control his entry to go either shallow or deep at will.

If he has any natural inclination towards diving, then this early introduction will have whetted his appetite for further advancement in the more specific art of diving for its own sake.

The First Obstacle The teaching of diving is regarded as a rather specialized art and is wrapped in mystery as far as the average person is concerned. To understand the reason for this difficulty, we must ask ourselves what is the obstacle to progress? What is required in diving that is not required in swimming?

Basically it is the fact that it is possible to swim without ever putting the face in the water – but, it is not possible to dive without putting the head completely under the water. The obstacle is *fear*, in this case fear of putting the head under water; fear in fact of drowning.

Self-preservation Every child has an inherent instinct of self-preservation, the desire to stay alive. Putting the head under the water interferes with the very process that keeps us alive – breathing! Any activity that interfers with this natural process of breathing will be instinctively resisted. If a child is to be taught to dive then this natural instinct must be broken down gradually before a successful attempt can be made to perform even the simplest head-first entry from the side.

Unfortunately, diving means to most people an activity at the *deep end* of the pool and so the reluctant child is taken there and asked to dive in head first, often with painful results.

Early Fears A young beginner cannot be expected to believe that if he dives head first into the deep water he will be able to survive for the time he is submerged, and also that he will come up again. He cannot imagine how it is possible for him to return to the surface, nor how it is possible not to be hurt by hitting the bottom. He cannot be expected to know that the water will slow his descent and that he would in fact have great difficulty in reaching the bottom in deep water. When asked of what is he afraid, he may not know; he is simply scared. His fears cannot be reasoned away, he must be given the opportunity to prove to himself that his fears are groundless.

Familiarity Brings Confidence The problems to be overcome will be better appreciated if we can understand the fears present in the child's mind. Our aim then is to eliminate these fears by subjecting the child to little doses of the very thing that is causing the fear until he becomes acclimatized. In this way we instil confidence into the child. The body very soon learns to adapt itself to these gradually changing conditions until the child is able to survive in them.

Fear of the unknown inhibits progress, whilst knowledge brings with it confidence. We must analyse the child's fears and give him the opportunity to discover exactly what will happen at each stage in the learning process. Ignorance can produce a state of panic; knowledge drives out fear; and familiarity brings confidence. As he becomes familiar with the conditions through repetition, the body and mind will react accordingly and make the necessary adjustments to cope with the changing conditions. Fear will gradually be eliminated as the body becomes acclimatized. Further repetition produces a state of adaptation. The body is then able to adjust automatically so that the diver is able to free his mind to concentrate on the specific skill being taught.

Eliminating Fear In the first instance it is the fear of putting the face, the breathing apparatus, into the water. The child must get used to having water on the face, putting the face in the water and holding the breath and breathing out under water. The child should be given the opportunity to get used to the increasing pressure of deep water as the body is submerged. He must also learn to appreciate the upthrust of the water that makes it difficult both to stay under water, and to hit the bottom hard.

He should be given the opportunity to get used to being upside down in water before he is asked to dive in head first. He must be encouraged to open his eyes under water: to see is to be less afraid. At the first attempts to open the eyes under water it may 'sting' (if only psychologically), but the beginner soon realizes that each time this happens, the next time becomes easier.

Preparing for the Entry The would-be diver must be taught to glide from the surface to the bottom of the pool to prepare for the most difficult part of the dive for a beginner – the entry into the water. Both teacher and pupil must appreciate the necessity of having the eyes open, and the hands in front for protection during the glide to the bottom. The descent to the bottom must be practised until the beginner appreciates the buoyancy of the water and the resultant resistance to the body's descent. The pupil must become fully accustomed to being near the bottom of the pool and to touching it with both hands.

Before embarking on any type of diving programme, it is therefore necessary that certain basic requirements are met. The would-be diver must be quite happy under water. He should be able to descend to the bottom in a depth of 8 feet (2.44 m) quite easily. He must also be quite used to being upside down in water and be able to keep his eyes open whenever he is below the surface. He should be able to balance on his hands in shallow water with ease.

Flight Problems The next problem the young beginner has to overcome is the transition from the side of the pool to the water i.e. the take-off and flight. This involves the act of overbalancing and falling, and immediately a new fear situation is created. This stage usually causes difficulty to both teacher and pupil. The degree of difficulty experienced will depend largely on the amount of preparatory work that has been accomplished.

It is very important that the eyes should be kept open during this stage. The diver should 'spot' the entry point on the surface and focus on it for as long as possible. The visual feedback to the brain will result in increased confidence when further attempts are made. When the diver loses contact with the side he is in a state of free fall (the flight) and further fear reactions may be triggered off, unless he has been prepared for it. The fear experienced will usually increase with a rise in the height of the take-off point.

Fear of Falling A young beginner about to enter head first from the side is being asked to do something that would cause him injury if performed on land. He is asked to fall forward and duck his head. If he fell forward on land, his natural reaction would be to lift his head up to avoid injury.

The fear of falling is an instinctive one present in most people. When a beginner is asked to learn forward and dive in head first, he starts off with every intention of doing so, then panics, perhaps subconsciously, and instinctively raises his head and falls flat on his stomach – the well known 'belly flop'. This is caused solely by fear, and not by any lack of knowledge or of technique.

To overcome this fear, the brain must be gradually conditioned to accept the unnatural action of falling and ducking the head. This is achieved by first learning to duck the head when already in the water where there is no falling required. Progression is by way of easy stages, gradually introducing the falling requirement until it causes no fear reaction. By analysing these fears we are able to recognize them and take the necessary action to dispel them. This takes time, and the earlier it is started the easier it will be to progress in diving.

Progressive Practice   These early fears can be eliminated in the *shallow end* of the bath during the normal swimming lesson. If a child is given the opportunity to progress through graduated structured material then diving will present no problems. A question that arises frequently is 'How long should one continue with a particular practice before going on to the next?'

The guiding factor is the *position of the head*. If the head can be held down, i.e. with the chin tucked in, then usually the essential require-ment is being complied with for that particular skill. A simple example is the Mushroom or Tuck float. If this cannot be performed with the head held down, then the person should not progress to the next more difficult skill. On the other hand, when the position can be held with the head well down for at least five seconds, then that skill has served its purpose.

The Method of Teaching   When a new practice is being attempted for the first time it is important to ensure that the diver knows where he is going at the *completion* of it. If he is to make a confident attempt he must know exactly what he is letting himself in for: there must be no doubt in his mind. In practice this means working backwards from the entry to the take-off. He must first get used to the entry requirements of the particular dive, then when the first elementary flight attempts are made the diver knows where he is going – he has 'been there before' so he is *confident*.

This is very important during the very early stages when first learning to dive. Having got used to the underwater part of the entry, the transition from the sitting position on the side into the water should not present any real difficulty.

Once having mastered the actual transition into the water from the sitting position, the diver can then work 'backwards', gradually increas-ing the duration of the flight by increasing the height of the body at take-off until the upright standing position is reached. The take-off movements can then be attempted with confidence. In this way only one new element is added at the *beginning* each time. Once he has taken off, that is, left the side, he knows where he is going. A young beginner not happy at entering the water head first will not be able to concentrate on the take-off, as all his thoughts will be on protecting himself when he hits the water.

The Feeler   A pupil's first attempt at a new skill is usually an explora-tory attempt called a 'feeler'. The body is being given a chance to experience the skill so that the brain can make the necessary adjustments to enable the skill to be performed correctly. The purpose of the first attempt at the skill is to set the fear mechanism at rest, i.e. to give a degree of confidence. When the brain is convinced that no harm will attend the execution of the skill, the inhibitions (the brakes) will be removed, and the 'performer' is ready to 'have a go' with confidence.

A diver should *never* be forced to attempt a dive before he is ready. The more courageous may be able to convince themselves *before* the attempt that no harm will befall them and so the first attempt may be a good one. On the other hand, another person may be more conscious of danger and so will make only a timid first attempt.

During the early attempts at a skill there is a continual conflict between the diver's physical and mental states. The more time the diver has in which to complete the dive the easier it will be to accomplish. Height alone provides time, but this requires extreme confidence at take-off. The nearer the diver is to the water at take-off, the easier the dive will be mentally as there will be less fear felt. But, a lower take-off position makes it more difficult to accomplish physically because there is less time available in which to do it. As confidence increases the dive can be attempted from a higher take-off position and so becomes easier to accomplish.

The State of Readiness   The wise teacher balances physical preparation with mental readiness, suggesting practices that can be attempted with confidence at each stage in the learning process. The teacher should have a string of progressive practices to choose from, selecting those that suit the physical ability and mental readiness of the pupil *at that particular moment*. The more timid pupils may need to go through the whole gamut of progressions, whereas the less nervous types may be able to start half-way up the ladder and miss a few progressions on the way. When the pupil is *ready*, that is the time to make the attempt. The experienced teacher is able to recognize this state of readiness and act accordingly.

Fear and Progress   Assuming a diver is receiving the correct instruction his progress will depend mainly on two things. First, the amount of *fear* experienced and secondly the amount of *natural ability* the diver possesses. There is an element of danger in diving which causes a normal fear reaction. Correctly structured material will do a great deal to inhibit fear, but in spite of this, some people are naturally more afraid than others and will obviously progress at a slower rate. These people need a more sympathetic approach if they are to show progress.

Natural Ability   Diving is a skilful sport requiring a high degree of neuro-muscular co-ordination. Some people have this developed to a greater degree than others so will progress much faster. Those with a high degree of natural ability may only need to *see* a new dive in order to be able to make a successful first attempt. Those with very little ability may find it difficult to translate a visual impression into a physical act and will need the utmost assistance from an understanding teacher if they are to progress.

It is possible for a diver with a high degree of physical ability to be very timid, and likewise for a diver with very little physical ability to have no fear. Both can show progress, but the scared diver with little physical ability is hardly likely to get very far. The diver with natural ability who has little fear will obviously show the greatest progress.

Learning Diving into water head first is not a natural act for a human being to perform, so unless the diver is taught, he may never learn how to do it correctly. Once learnt, however, the skill is not forgotten and constant practice is not then necessary to retain it. This applies to diving at any level. Regular and frequent practice is necessary during the *learning* process but directly the skill can be performed consistently, it becomes a subconscious activity and from then on can be performed without thought. It has been learnt.

Practice with Guidance It is important during the learning process that the skill is performed under the guidance of the teacher to prevent bad habits forming. It is sometimes useful for the pupils to work in pairs or groups, one helping the other. This is not only helpful to the performer but also of assistance to the helper who acquires a greater insight into the skill to his own benefit later on. This method of pairing also frees the teacher handling large groups, allowing him to concentrate on those who need his help.

It is very difficult for a diver to know exactly how he has performed a dive, especially in the early attempts. During this period it is necessary for someone with knowledge to be on hand to convey this information to him. The brain cannot tell 'right' from 'wrong', it can only consolidate that which is practised, so it is essential that the skill is practised correctly for it is just as easy to learn it incorrectly as correctly.

Personal Performance of the Teacher It is not necessary for the teacher of diving to be able to perform the dives he teaches, although, obviously, to speak from experience would give him extra confidence. With the technical knowledge available today it is, however, quite possible to teach diving to a fairly high level without being a competent performer oneself. There is, however, no substitute for personal experience and the teacher is strongly advised to practise as far as possible.

The activities outlined in Chapters 5 and 6 are well within the capabilities of any teacher. All teachers of diving should go through those activities to gain a greater insight into them. It is then possible to visualize the dive when teaching it. The descriptions are written in the first person for this reason.

By means of this personal practice one can appreciate the difficulties and problems that beset the young beginner, and therefore tend to have a more tolerant attitude and more sympathetic approach to teaching this subject. Although the non-diving teacher may never aspire to performing an Inward or Reverse Dive he can practise the essential requirements of the take-off in the privacy of his home if necessary.

Skill   Skill is basically a learned response. Practice enables a person to become skilled at a particular movement. It is generally recognized that skill is *specific*. We cannot learn to be skilful, nor acquire a general faculty of skill. We can only become skilful at a particular movement through practice of that movement. If two movements are similar, however, practice of one *may* assist in the learning of the other, but transfer of training is not automatic.

Diving is technically a 'closed skill' sport, that is, it can be practised anywhere in its entirety, there are no *extraneous* circumstances to be taken into consideration at a later date. This means that each dive may be learned and used as a stepping stone towards the learning of the next dive in its group. In a sport such as tennis, although the basic require-ments of the individual skills may be learned, the conditions in an actual game are dependent to a large extent on the skill of one's opponent. The tennis player must be ready for any and every eventuality, he does not know what he is required to do until just before having to do it. We call this sort of sport an 'open skill' sport.

Kinaesthetic Sense   During any physical activity the brain receives continual feedback signals from the various sense organs in use, such as those of sight, sound and touch, so that we are aware of our position in the external environment. It also receives *internal* feedback signals from the joints, muscle fibres and muscle tendons, so that we know exactly where each limb is in relation to its neighbour, and also how much tension there is in the muscles responsible for the movement of the limbs about the joints. This enables us to assume specific body positions even with our eyes closed. Messages from the delicate organs of balance in the inner ear also keep the brain informed of the general body position so that we can maintain our equilibrium at all times.

Some pupils have a greater kinaesthetic sense or body awareness than others. They can feel every body position; they do not need to see. Others may only be able to assume a position correctly providing they can see their limbs. Unfortunately we cannot *teach* this, as it is part of the body's physiological make-up. It is inherited. We can only try to make the diver aware of his body and make him think of what he is doing in the hope that it will awaken some dormant ability.

Consistency As a result of the feedback signals received, the brain sends messages to the various muscles to produce the required movement. This is a highly complicated neuro-muscular act, and can be performed most efficiently by the more gifted person. Those persons with a finely co-ordinated stimulus-response mechanism will be able to evoke the same response every time for a given stimulus. They have consistency. These fortunate beings are able to repeat an act exactly, whilst others may need two or three attempts to produce the desired result. In any sport with an element of danger in it, consistency is a very important safety requirement. In competitive diving it is the hallmark of the champion.

The more gifted divers are able to visualize a complete dive in the mind, and can 'feel' their way through the movements mentally. This is obviously a valuable asset and will facilitate the learning process. To be able to do this, the diver must first know how a particular dive looks when it is performed correctly. He then aims to execute the dive as he sees it and so feel, physically, the correct movements.

Having acquired the feel of the dive performed well, he then has something to aim for every time he attempts that particular dive.

Obstacles to Progress As the diver becomes more proficient and attempts new dives the teacher should be aware of three obstacles which may retard further progress. These are:

1. *Ignorance* of what is required. This is usually caused through insufficient explanation and lack of demonstration by the teacher, and is inexcusable.

The experienced teacher readily appreciates the old saying,

To *hear* is to *forget*
To *see* is to *understand*
To *do* is to *know*.

2. *Pain* experienced through striking the water awkwardly or hitting the side of the bath or end of the board. The wise teacher tries to avoid this happening by the use of structured material.

3. *Fear* of possible injury. This can be minimized by correct teaching.

Ignorance It is very easy for a teacher who knows the work thoroughly to take too much for granted, assuming that the pupil understands what he is saying. It is imperative when teaching any activity with an element of danger in it that the pupil *understands* precisely what he is expected to do.

A good practical demonstration has more impact and conveys more information than any verbal description. A verbal description has to be translated by the diver into a visual picture. Some are more gifted in this than others. In extreme cases it may not be possible for a diver to visualize what is required even from the most lucid description. Ideally a live demonstration will convey the most impact. Next, a film especially if in slow motion, is invaluable. But failing this, a demonstration using a flexible figure with the necessary explanations will usually convey the correct picture.

Pain No diver should be allowed to experience a painful smack on the water at entry. If this happens more than once it is extremely unlikely that the diver will attempt to dive again for some time. Ideally the diver should be made to do the dive again *as soon as possible* otherwise a psychological block will build up which will prevent any further attempts at that particular dive. He may lose his nerve unless he makes another attempt at the same dive during that session.

The same applies to hitting the board. This may happen particularly with Reverse and Inward Dives. The teacher or coach must be sure that he has knowledge of the mechanics of the dive being taught. Both teacher and coach must be fully confident that they know the essential techniques required to ensure that the diver clears the board safely, and that the diver also knows them and is capable of putting them into practice.

In spite of a teacher having the knowledge and taking every precaution, accidents do occur. This sometimes happens when a diver is not feeling fit or he loses his concentration. Some divers haven't the degree of consistency required for the execution of difficult dives and for no apparent reason will do something entirely out of context.

Training sessions should not continue to the point where a diver is becoming tired or fatigued. This is when accidents are most likely to happen.

The Greatest Obstacle – Fear Diving is an activity that lends itself to being broken down into easily teachable elements. Although dives progress in increments of a half somersault there comes a time when the step from one to another is too great. *Fear* prevents further progress and until this can be eliminated no improvement is possible. This often occurs when a diver, having learnt a Forward Somersault, attempts a $1\frac{1}{2}$ Somersault or having learnt a Back Somersault attempts a $1\frac{1}{2}$ Back Somersault. Although he may know exactly what he is required to do to execute the dive correctly, he finds that he just cannot bring himself to do it. A *mental* block prevents any physical action.

Eliminating fear is a process of overcoming, i.e. inhibiting, a natural psychological emotion.

If fear can be eliminated from a diver's mind, *anything* is possible. Everything the teacher or coach does must be directed towards this end – the removing of the greatest obstacle to progress in diving – fear.

5. First Steps in Diving

The first steps in diving are the most important and can, if carried out correctly, make the subsequent learning process much easier to accomplish. These early practices should normally be introduced during the general swimming lessons in the comparative safety of shallow water. As general swimming ability improves progress can be made to deeper water. These activities can be grouped conveniently under three main headings, i.e. Submerging, Gliding and Springing practices.

SUBMERGING PRACTICES

The object of the submerging practices is to:
  I. Develop breath-holding ability.
  II. Enable the eyes to remain open under water.
  III. Appreciate the buoyancy force (upthrust) of water.
  IV. Introduce the body to the inverted position.

1. Ducking *(Fig. 3)*   Stand in the shallow water, feet slightly apart with your body bent forward and your hands on your knees. Take a normal breath, close your mouth and press your face under the water. See how long you can hold your breath before raising your head and breathing out. If you have never done this before it may seem an alarming thing to do, but persevere because it is essential that you master it. Each time you do it you will find it easier, as the body adapts itself remarkably quickly to the face being under the water. Try to relax and open your eyes. When you can do this easily, try it again but this time after holding your breath, exhale blowing bubbles until all your air is exhausted before raising your head.

2. Picking up Objects *(Fig. 4)*   Now that you can duck your head and open your eyes easily under water, you are ready to put your new-found ability to the test. It is time for you to try to pick up an object from the bottom of the bath. When you become proficient you can try to pick up pennies from the bottom, but it is better to use something large enough for you to grasp hold of easily for the first few attempts. The rubber life-saving brick to be found at most baths is very suitable.

If the water is deep you may find it quite a struggle at first and may only be able to grasp it with one hand. Keep on trying until you are able to get right to the bottom and can grasp it with both hands.

Fig. 3. Ducking   Fig. 4. Picking up objects   Fig. 5. Hands on the bottom

3. Hands on the Bottom (*Fig. 5*)   You are now ready to attempt to place both hands flat on the bottom. To do this, you must get your hips above your head. Try kicking your legs out of the water. Your legs will not be supported by the water and their weight will help you stay down long enough for you to get your hands in position.

4. Floating Face Down (*Fig. 6*)   After trying to pick up objects from the bottom you will soon realize that it is difficult to sink in water because the water exerts a force upwards against you. If you get down into the water it will support you. You are now ready to try to float in it, in the three recognized body positions used in diving.

Fig. 6. Floating face down

The easiest to try is the *Tuck* float. Stand in shallow water, bend forward and put your hands on your knees then press your head down into the water. As your head goes down your feet will lift off the bottom, then draw your knees up tightly, holding on to them with your hands. You will now be floating in a tight tuck position with just part of your back out of the water. For this reason it is usually called 'the mushroom float'.

The next position to try is the *Pike* float. Start as before but instead of bending your knees, sit back slightly and reach down with your hands to touch your toes. Before you reach your toes, your feet will rise forward to meet your hands, and you will be floating with just part of your back out of the water as before.

Plate 5. Tuck Float   *Plate 6. Pike Float*

The *Straight* float face downwards is the next position to try. Start as if you were going to perform a Tuck float, but as your feet float off the bottom bend your knees and raise your feet *behind* you at the same time stretch your hands in front of you. When you feel yourself floating in this position stretch your legs so that you are floating just under the surface with your body fully extended. This is the position that you will aim for when you start your gliding practices.

This is a difficult position to maintain so don't worry if your legs start to sink. As long as you get the feeling of lying stretched out in the water you will have achieved your object. You might like to test your skill by performing a Tuck float then stretching into a Straight float. If you can go into a Straight float from a Pike float then you are doing extremely well. Don't forget that in all these exercises your face should be in the water. You are now ready to glide.

GLIDING PRACTICES

The gliding practices are designed to:

I. Introduce the leg push required for the *take-off*.

II. Develop the stretched and streamlined body position required for the *entry*.

III. Ensure that the hands are kept extended beyond the head for *protection* when travelling head first under water.

IV. Accustom the body to descending head first towards the bottom with the eyes open.

Fig. 7. Gliding on the surface

1. Gliding on the Surface *(Fig. 7)*   Stand in chest-deep water with your back to the side of the bath. Bend forward, put your face in the water and open your eyes. Then place both feet on the wall behind you and push off vigorously so that you glide along the surface with your arms extended beyond your head, hands clasped together thumbs interlocked, palms facing forward (see Fig. 8).

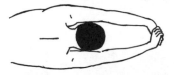

Fig. 8. Flat-hand entry technique

Your legs should be straight with feet together, and *toes pointed*. You should aim to stretch the whole body, making it as firm and as straight as possible.

Glide as far as you can, watching the bottom of the bath then press down with your hands. At the same time raise your head, bend your knees and place your feet on the bottom. Check how far you travel and try to improve on it at each new attempt. Keep a note of your attempts and whether you are able to keep your eyes open the whole time. Are you able to glide without rolling sideways? Are you able to keep your feet together with toes pointed and body stretched? Are you able to keep your arms extended in front, hands clasped together?

2. Gliding to the Bottom – Float Up *(Fig. 9)*   When you are able to glide easily on the surface your next aim is to glide towards the bottom. Start as before, but in order to reach the bottom you must direct your body downwards as you push off. You do this by keeping your head down. Your head acts as a rudder under water – where your head goes the body follows. Keep your eyes open, watch for the bottom and reach in front with your hands to protect your head. As you near the bottom

Fig. 9. Gliding to the bottom, floating up

raise your head and tilt your hands upwards, and you will glide to the surface. This is a good exercise to increase your breath-holding ability.

3. Gliding to the Bottom – Push Up *(Fig. 10)*   Repeat the glide to the bottom but this time aim to touch the bottom with your hands. Directly you touch, press down with your hands, raise your head, bend your knees and place your feet on the bottom. Push off vigorously with your feet and see how high you can rise above the surface. This is the method divers use to get to the surface quickly in deep water. Next, experiment by aiming for specific points on the bottom, say the lane lines, trying to touch one with your hands before surfacing. Try touching the line nearest to the side. This will require a much steeper angle

Plate 7. Gliding to the bottom   *Plate 8. Pushing off from the bottom*

of descent and you will now find it more important that you keep your hands in front for protection.

Fig. 10. Gliding to the bottom, pushing up

4. Surface Dive to Balance *(Fig. 11)* The surface dive is a worthwhile skill to master, as, apart from its value in enabling you to get used to the vertical entry positions for diving, it is used in many other aquatic sports.

Fig. 11. Surface dive to balance

Push off and glide on the surface, then sweep your arms sideways, at the same time duck your head and bend at the hips. When your head is below your hips raise your legs and place your hands on the bottom. Try to hold the balance. At first you will find it easier to bend your legs at the knees in order to get them up vertically above your hips. As you become more proficient, aim to keep your legs straight and together until you touch the bottom with your hands. With practice you will be able to hold the position balanced on your hands for a few seconds. It is now even more important that you keep your arms extended beyond your head. The more vertical you get your body the quicker you will go to the bottom. *Keep your eyes open and arms in front of your head.* When you can do the surface dive with ease you will have come a long way to getting yourself ready for your first head-first dive. Your next task, however, is to attempt to push off from the bottom instead of the side wall of the bath and land on your hands as in the surface dive. In the surface dive, your body rotated through 90° from horizontal to vertical. Pushing off from a standing position to touch the bottom with your hands requires the body to rotate through 180°; this is much more difficult.

SPRINGING PRACTICES

The springing practices are designed to:

I. Introduce the body movements required to produce *rotation* at take off.

II. Develop the leg drive necessary to obtain *height* at take-off.

III. Accustom the body to taking the weight on the hands in the inverted position in order to *protect the head* on entry.

1. Crouch Spring to Touch Bottom *(Fig. 12)*   Stand in chest-deep water, body bent forwards at the hips, legs bent at the knees, arms above the head, eyes focused on the bottom.

Spring up, aiming to push your hips out of the water. At the same time duck your head, and dig your hands into the water in front of your head. Keep your eyes open and look for the bottom reaching for it with both hands. When you have touched the bottom press your head back and push away with your hands and continue up to the surface. If you are not able to do this easily, check that you are maintaining the hips-bent position during the leg push. The aim is to push your hips above the the surface. When you can do this every time with confidence you are ready to try pushing off with your feet.

Fig. 12. Crouch Spring to touch the bottom

2. Crouch Spring and Push Off *(Fig. 13)*   Take off as before, pushing hard with your feet to drive your hips up. Reach for the bottom with your hands. When your hands touch the bottom lift your head and

Fig. 13. Crouch Spring and push off

push with your hands as before but this time bend your legs at the knees and place your feet on the bottom. Push off vigorously with your feet and see how high you can jump out of the water. Repeat this until you can place your hands on the bottom with confidence every time.

3. Crouch Spring to Balance *(Fig. 14)* Take up exactly the same position as before, but this time you must push harder at take off, and duck your head more forcibly so that your hips rise up above your head. Reach for the bottom, place your hands firmly on the bottom and try to maintain the position balanced on your hands. You will probably find it easier if you keep your legs bent at the knees until your hands are on the bottom in a crouch position then see how high you can spring out your legs to the vertical. Experiment with your head position while in the balance. Pressing the head backwards will prevent your overbalancing while pressing the chin on to the chest will do the opposite, that is, make you overbalance, or more important, bring you into balance if you feel you cannot quite make it. To perform this on dry land would be quite a gymnastic feat. Water enables you to perform easily many gymnastic skills that you would find very difficult to do in a gymnasium. If you can accomplish this with ease then you may like to try it with legs held straight after take-off.

Fig. 14. Crouch Spring to balance

Fig. 15. Pike Spring to balance

4. Pike Spring to Balance *(Fig. 15)*   Start as for the Crouch Spring, but after the spring, keep your legs straight throughout until you are balanced on your hands. This will require a little more effort at take-off. Make sure that you push your hips up vigorously to create the rotation needed. When you are able to do this easily, you are well on the way to entering head first from the side. You have actually performed the take-off, flight and entry movements required in the Plain Header.

KEEPING THE FUN IN THE FUNDAMENTALS

Having mastered the fundamentals of diving, here are a few activities that you can enjoy along with your friends.

1. Flying Porpoise   Perform a Crouch Spring and Push Off as in Fig. 13, but as you spring up out of the water bend at the hips, duck your head and dive towards the bottom again performing another Crouch Spring and Push Off. This can be performed across the bath by repeat-it continuously. You can challenge your friends starting from the shallow end working towards the deep end to see who can go the farthest.

2. Over the Hands   Two partners hold hands facing one another. You stand close to their hands and perform a Crouch Spring and dive over their hands without touching them. The partners can hold their hands below the surface, on the surface or above the surface according to your ability.

3. Through the Ring   Get two of your friends to hold hands, arms apart, forming a 'ring'. Tip the ring up so they each have one hand in the water and one in the air directly above. You then dive through the ring trying not to touch their hands. If you cannot quite make it, they just help you on your way by lifting your legs with their lower arms – without breaking their grip.

4. Between the Legs   Your partner stands with his feet wide apart facing you. You perform a Crouch Spring and glide between his legs.

5. Over the Back   You bend forward with your hands on your knees and your friend stands at your side with his hands on your back. He springs up, takes his hands away and dives over your back to the bottom.

6. Touching Feet   Your partner stands with his feet apart whilst you dive down to touch both his feet.

7. Counting Fingers It is important that we always open our eyes underwater. To encourage this in the early stages, swimmers work in pairs, one holding a hand below the surface with a set number of fingers extended. The other ducks under and counts them. This can be done with small coloured objects such as plastic discs or clothes pegs. The object is clasped in a closed fist until the partner submerges his face. He names the colour displayed.

8. Sitting on the Bottom When you try this exercise you may find difficulty in getting to the bottom, if so, try jumping up first, lifting your feet out of the water and bending at the hips, at the same time leaning back slightly. If you breathe out slowly you will find it easier to stay down.

9. Jumping In Besides being a quick and easy way of entering the water, jumping in will give you confidence and also prepare you for the feet-first entries that you will be learning at a later stage. These jumps should be free and informal, paying no attention to the style. When you first try them into shallow water, bend your knees and land with your feet apart to avoid any jar to your body. After a few attempts you will find that you will do it automatically. Then try it with a run . . . see how far out you can go, then see how high you can get. Next jump backwards, then try jumping in forwards and turning round to face the side before you enter the water.

By now you are becoming quite an expert, so try jumping in landing on the bottom in a crouch position then see how high you can spring out of the water. You are now ready to try jumping in without your feet touching the bottom. How? Well, one way is to lift your feet up as you jump. See how many other ways you can think of! Diving in head first from the side requires deeper water so your next aim is to get used to being in deep water.

DEEP-WATER PRACTICES

Before attempting to enter head first from the side, there are one or two preparatory exercises that you should perform in *deeper* water to acclimatize you to the depth of water into which you intend to dive.

1. Deep-water Jumps This is a good way to get used to the deep water. First, jump in, bending your knees as you land on the bottom, then give a good push off to see how quickly you can rise to the surface. If the water is deeper than 8 feet (2.5 m) you may find it difficult to touch the bottom, because of the upthrust of the water opposing your descent.

The straighter and more vertical you keep your body on entry the deeper you will descend. This will also increase your speed to the bottom, so be extra careful in shallow water otherwise you may stub your toes. Point your toes as you enter the water, but flatten your feet below the surface.

Water up the Nose   You may find difficulty in preventing water entering your nose when you jump in. If you do, try breathing in just as you jump. The extra air pressure inside your lungs should prevent water entering your nose. If it still persists in entering the nose, blow out through your nose as your head goes under.

Pressure on the Ears   When you first descend upside down into deep water you experience increased pressure on your ears. Depending on how clear your head is, and how much practice you have put in with your jumps into deep water, you may not experience any discomfort.

As you go deeper, the water pressure increases, and you may find your ears hurt. This is because the Eustachian tube connecting the middle ear with the nose is blocked, so that air at increased pressure cannot get through to balance the increased water pressure on the outside of the ear drum. Immediately you feel any pain, try swallowing, or moving the chin from side to side, or pinching the nose and blowing *gently* to clear the tubes, whilst still underwater. As your body gets used to repeated submergings in deep water, it will adapt itself automatically to open up the tubes. *Never* go deep if you have a cold or any sort of sinus infection, as the infection may be carried along to the middle ear with unpleasant results.

2. Deep-water Glide to the Bottom   Repeat the exercise in Fig. 9 in deep water. Aim to glide down to the bottom at an angle of 45° to the surface. By gliding down at this angle the increase in pressure is spread over a longer period of time. It is a more gradual process than if you were to dive down vertically. It may not be possible for you to reach the bottom at this angle in very deep water. If not, raise your head and return to the surface when you have gone as deep as you can manage comfortably. When you are quite happy with this try again but increase the angle of descent so that you go down at an angle of about 60° to the surface. If you manage to get near to the bottom hang on, then tuck up and push off as in Fig. 10. This will get you to the surface much quicker than swimming up.

3. Deep-water Surface Dive   Your next task is to try a surface dive (Fig. 11) in deep water. If you are able to execute a surface dive with legs straight and vertical with knees well above the surface then you will descend deep and will reach the increased pressure much quicker.

You will, however, be conditioned to it by now so should experience no discomfort at all. You should be able to touch the bottom at a depth of 8 feet (2.44 m) with ease. You will only touch the bottom gently because your downward momentum will be almost completely absorbed. If you wish to return to the surface at any time during the descent, pull your hands down in front of your body, raise your head and tuck your legs up beneath you. Your body will now rotate backwards so that your feet are below your head. If you are near the bottom just put your feet down and push up to the surface. You are now experiencing the feel of a head-first entry into deep water. When you come to dive from the side you will have no fear of entering the water.

6. *Basic Bathside Work*

Providing the practices described in Chapter 5 have been worked through, there should now be very little difficulty in teaching the head-first entry from the side into deeper water. At some stage, however, the teacher may find that unfortunately one or two pupils in the group have not received this essential early training. If it is not possible for them to go back to the shallow-water practices, the teacher must find some other method of bridging the gap from the water to the bathside.

In cases of this sort the deep-water practices outlined in Chapter 5 should be practised very throughly before venturing in head first from the side. The teacher must ensure that the pupil can descend to the bottom in deep water with confidence.

The basic bathside work is divided into Sitting, Kneeling, and Standing Dives. The complete list of bathside practices given in this chapter may be followed through with the more timid pupils. For the pupils who have received a good grounding in the shallow-water exercises of Chapter 5, the teacher will select from the list exercises appropriate to their needs. For example, with the less timid pupils one could start with the 'Sitting Dives', leave out the whole of the 'Kneeling Dives' section and progress to the 'Standing Dives'. With the more timid pupil, the kneeling group will provide a more gradual transition from sitting to standing, giving the opportunity to overcome many inherent fears. Many teachers of diving pass too quickly through the sitting dive stage. The experienced teacher will know that time spent here will greatly facilitate the transition to the standing dive.

Individual Problems   Individual pupils have their own peculiar problems and may find that certain progressions suit them, whilst other pupils may find the same exercise awkward or difficult to accomplish successfully. The wise teacher will give his pupils the opportunity of trying out as many different methods of entering the water as possible, leaving them to decide which one suits them at any particular moment.

Preparing for the Entry   When you have taken up your starting position, focus your eyes on the water surface at the point you aim to enter. Watch the entry point until your hands touch the water, then duck your head between your arms to ensure that the top of your head enters first, not your face. With each exercise it is important that you get the top of your head into the water first, before you proceed to the next exercise. If you find that you are lifting your head as you enter, then return to the previous exercise.

Make sure you know exactly what each exercise should look and feel like when it is performed correctly. Practise it a number of times until you can do it well before passing on to the next one. In this way you will progress with confidence and your performance will be consistent.

Entry Requirements When entering the water head first you must always ensure that:

I. The hands are clasped together, with thumbs interlocked, one hand clamped over the other, palms facing forward, arms extended in front to protect the head (see Fig. 8).

II. The eyes are opened as soon as possible under water, to see the bottom.

III. A slight forward bend at the hips is maintained on entry to prevent injury to the back. (Never arch the back on entry.)

In your first attempts at any head-first dive, aim to enter the water at an angle of about 45°. This provides a longer path to the bottom: very important in shallow water, and makes surfacing much easier. As you become more proficient you can make your angle of entry steeper, about 60° to 80° to the surface. Reach for the bottom, place both hands on the bottom taking the weight on your arms.

Surfacing Techniques When you are completely submerged in deep water you may arch your back, pull down with your hands and swim up to the surface. To surface from a near vertical entry in deep water pull your arms straight down in front of your body, at the same time tucking up so that you rotate backwards, finishing with your feet beneath you. If you are near to the bottom, place your feet on the bottom and push up to the surface. If not, then stretch and swim up.

SITTING DIVES

Before attempting to dive in from a standing position, make sure that you can enter confidently from a sitting position. *For Sitting Dives you need water as deep as your own height up to your chin.* In pools where there is no rail or trough it may not be possible to perform the exercise exactly as described. In this case the feet should be placed flat on the side of the wall if possible. In pools where the surface of the water is very near to the pool surround level, the Kneeling Dives can be attempted in place of the Sitting Dives.

1. Low Sitting Fall *(Fig. 16)* Sit on the side as far back as possible with your feet placed firmly on the trough or rail. Bend downwards towards the water with your head between your arms, hands clasped together in front, until your fingers touch the water. Having got yourself in position, reach down towards the bottom and allow yourself to overbalance slowly. Keep your head down between your arms, push with your feet and enter the water without any splash. Aim to enter the water at an angle of about 45° and when you are completely submerged, and not until then, raise your head and glide up to the surface. When you are able to do this confidently, try the next progression.

Plate 9. Entry from a Sitting Dive

Keep your head down and reach for the bottom with your hands. Try to balance on the bottom in a tuck balance position as you did in the water practices.

A common fault is to drop in knees first. Just as the balance is lost and the feeling of falling is experienced you lose confidence and try to jump in. If this happens then go back to the previous activities. If you still find this dive difficult then try the sitting dive from the top of the steps with your feet on the next step down. At first you may find that you have your knees bent as you enter the water, but don't let that worry you. The most important thing to remember is to keep the head down. Continue practising until you can straighten your knees and push your hips up as you roll forward. You should eventually be able to keep your legs straight all the way until you are in an armstand position on the bottom.

Fig. 16. Low Sitting Fall

Fig. 17. High Sitting Fall

2. High Sitting Fall *(Fig. 17)* Sit on the side as before but with your body more upright, bent forward about 45° from the vertical. Clasp your hands together with your arms straight and resting on your knees, and then topple forward slowly, ducking your head between your arms as your hands enter the water.

Plate 10. Sitting Fall position

Plate 11. Sitting Spring position

3. Sitting Spring *(Fig. 18)* Sit on the side as before, but this time sit upright with your arms extended above your head. Keeping your arms by your ears, bend forward towards the water at the same time straightening your legs and pushing your hips up. The spring as you take off will

Fig. 18. Sitting Spring

give you the feeling of flight. Enter the water at an angle of 45° gliding towards the bottom and trying to touch one of the black lines. Then try entering the water practically horizontal and see how far you are able to glide on the surface. This is very good practice for the dive you will use when you are entering the water for a swim. Don't forget to keep your head down all the time even when you are gliding on the surface.

These Sitting Dives are valuable because you can perform them in shallow water, so enabling you to learn to dive whilst you are learning to swim. When you can perform the Sitting Dive with arms up so that you are able to push up your hips and keep your legs straight, entering the water as shown in the accompanying figures, you will be able to progress to diving in from a standing position on the rail or trough.

KNEELING DIVES

The Kneeling Dives in this section also include the Squat and Lunge Dives, all requiring the feet to be separated, one on the edge, the other behind.

The minimum depth of water required is a depth equal to one's own height. There is little speed at entry, and if the entry is angled at 45°, it will provide an even greater margin of safety.

1. Kneeling Fall *(Fig. 19)*   Kneel on the side with the toes of one foot gripping the edge. The other knee must also be on the edge, level with the foot. By placing your knee on the edge, level with your foot, you spread your body weight evenly so that you can balance more easily throughout the movement. If you place your knee back from the edge you will probably find that you will not be able to support yourself on your foot during the start of the dive.

Bend forward so that your shoulder is touching your knee, reach down towards the water with your hands, pressing your head down between your arms. Let yourself overbalance slowly, reaching for the water with your hands – keep your *head down* and you should have no trouble in entering head first.

Fig. 19. Kneeling Fall

Plate 12. Squat position

2. Squat Fall *(Fig. 20)* Having mastered the Kneeling Fall, you are ready to raise yourself a little higher and start from a squatting position on the side. Take up the squat position with the toes of one foot gripping the edge and the toes of the other foot a little back from the edge by the heel of the forward foot. Bend forward keeping your head down, with your arms extended towards the water as before. Let yourself over-balance forwards as you reach for the water, then push with the front foot, entering the water at an angle of 45°. Try to straighten your legs and place your feet together with toes pointed before your hips go beneath the surface. Remember to keep your head down between your arms until your feet are in the water. When you are *completely* submerged you can think about the return to the surface – but not before.

Do you know why you put one foot slightly behind the other in the squat position? Try putting both feet together toes gripping the edge of the pool surround. What difference do you find? You should find it much easier to control your balance with one foot behind the other as it gives you a longer base, providing greater stability.

Fig. 20. Squat Fall

Fig. 21. Squat Spring

3. Squat Spring *(Fig. 21)* Take up the squat position as before but with your body more upright, bent forwards about 45° from the vertical, arms extended beyond your head. Bend down towards the water, at the same time raise your hips up behind and push from your feet and enter the water as before. The spring as you take off should enable you to get the same feeling of flight as in the Sitting Spring.

4. Lunge Dive *(Fig. 22)*   For this dive you start with one foot on the edge with the knee bent slightly and the other foot approximately 2 feet (0.60 m) behind. Bend downwards with your arms straight and your head between your arms. Overbalance forward, reaching towards the water with your hands, and at the same time lift the rear leg behind you. This acts as a counterweight allowing you to topple in slowly. As your hands touch the water, your take-off foot leaves the side and rises into position beside the other leg. As you overbalance forward, keep the rear leg low, about parallel with the side. A common fault is to let this leg kick up over the head and this must be avoided.

Fig. 22. Lunge Dive

STANDING DIVES

These are dives starting with both feet together, toes gripping the edge, heels down. The minimum depth of water required for the 'falls' is equal to one's own height, but for the 'springs' add an extra 12 inches (0.30 m).

Plate 13. Low Crouch position

1. Crouch Fall *(Fig. 23)*   Take up a low crouch position, body bent forward at the hips, knees bent. The feet may be together or slightly apart, heels down, toes gripping the edge. Clasp your hands together and tuck your head between your arms. Reach down until your hands are level with your feet. This is your starting position. Then reach down farther and overbalance slowly into the water gradually straightening your body, as you enter at an angle of about 45° to the surface. There must be no push, keep your toes in contact with the side as long as possible. When you can do this with confidence, try entering the water nearer to the side at an angle of about 60° to the surface.

Fig. 23. Crouch Fall

2. Plunge Fall   In addition to learning the near vertical entry required for diving you can now include practices to help you dive into the water to swim. The first time you stand on the side and achieve this is a memorable experience. The best way of entering the water in order to swim is by means of the Plunge. This is a very shallow dive, the body being nearly horizontal at entry so that it glides *along the surface* instead of to the bottom. You are now ready to attempt this. Take up the same starting position as you would for the Crouch Fall but this time 'spot' the entry about 6 feet (1.8 m) out from the side. Allow yourself to overbalance forward until your knees are nearly level with your feet; then push hard and your body will be projected forward in a more or less horizontal direction and you will enter the water at a very shallow angle. Keep your head down so that you glide just under the surface. Hold your position until you come to the surface and see how far you can travel before your feet start to sink.

3. Plunge Dive   The Plunge Dive follows on naturally from the gliding practices in Chapter 5 giving the body the experience of travelling faster through the water to develop further control at entry. Start again in the low crouch position, but this time with your hands touching the bathside, one each side of your feet. Overbalance as before, and swing your arms forward towards the entry point, pushing hard with your feet. You can then try starting with your arms behind you. This should enable you to glide farther.

4. Pike Fall *(Fig. 24)*   This is one of the most important exercises to master, and you cannot practise it too much. It can be used from all boards at any height with complete safety providing, of course, that you remember the golden rule of diving, never progress to a higher board if there is the slightest suggestion of your going over on entry.

Stand on the bathside bent forward in a deep pike position with your legs straight. Stretch your arms towards the water, clasping your hands together. Focus your eyes on the water at the point you expect to enter. Start to overbalance slowly, keeping your body bent at the hips so that your trunk is nearly vertical when your hands touch the water. As your body enters the water raise your legs slowly behind you until they are in line with your trunk.

You should perform this in a depth of water at least equal to your own height. If you have to perform in a lesser depth, adjust your angle of entry to suit the depth but always keep your hands above your head for protection. The important point to watch is that your body follows the line of flight, each part passing through the 'hole' made by your hands. When you try this for the first time you may find that, just as you are losing your balance and experiencing the feeling of falling, you want to

Plate 14. Pike Fall position   *Plate 15. Pike Fall Entry*

bend your knees and push with your feet. This is a natural reaction so don't let it worry you. A fear of falling is present in everyone and it is natural to try to save yourself by trying to get your feet in first. Much will depend on how well you have practised the Sitting Spring (Fig. 18). If you can perform this as described you should not have these difficulties. Keep your body bent slightly at the hips as you enter the water. On no account arch up until your feet are submerged otherwise you may injure your back.

Fig. 24. Pike Fall

5. Low Crouch Spring *(Fig. 25)*   Take up a low crouch position, body bent forward at the hips, knees bent. Clasp your hands together above your head, arms in line with your trunk. Focus your eyes on the spot where you expect to enter the water about 3 feet (1 m) from the side. This is your starting position. When you are ready, straighten your legs, push with your feet in order to drive your hips up high. Keep your body bent at the hips and you will have no difficulty in entering the water head first at the first attempt. As you enter you should straighten your body bringing the legs into line with the trunk. You will enter the water at an angle of about 60° to the surface and when you are completely submerged, you may raise your head and return to the surface. Practise this until you can do it every time with confidence. The object of starting in the crouch position is to ensure that the spring takes place *before* you

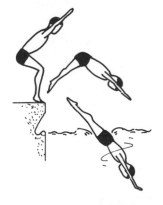

Fig. 25. Low Crouch Spring

have toppled too far. As you spring you will automatically start to overbalance in order to clear the side, but do not do it consciously. As you
become more confident, increase the strength of your push at take-off
but *never* allow yourself to go over on entry. This is a bad fault.

6. High Crouch Spring *(Fig. 26)*   As your confidence grows you
can start in a more upright position. Spring as before, pushing vigorously
with your feet. You should leave the side with your legs straight and
your toes pointed. Maintain the pike position, aiming to get your trunk
in vertically, bringing your legs into line as you submerge.

You should now be acquiring the flight feeling at the peak of the dive.
It feels as if you are 'suspended' for a brief moment. In order to get this
feeling your entry must not be too far out. Get someone to check your
feet as you leave the side. In a good take-off your feet should move back
over the side as they rise. If they move forward over the water then you
are allowing yourself to overbalance too much as you spring. Try not to
lean at all – just spring upwards.

Fig. 26. High Crouch Spring

7. Pike Spring *(Fig. 27)*   Start with your body bent forward at the
hips about 45° from the 'vertical' with your legs straight. Then move
your weight forward on to the balls of the feet and pause. All that you
need to do now is to bend at the knees, then, without pause, straighten
your legs and push with your feet. Keep bent at the hips until your hands
touch the water. Imagine that you are diving over a pole in front of your
hips, and push hard. Focus your eyes on the entry point and enter as
before.

Fig. 27. Pike Spring   *Fig. 28. Spring Header*

8. Spring Header *(Fig. 28)*   You are now ready to try your first real standing dive. Take up a position on the edge with your feet together, your legs straight, trunk bent forward slightly and your arms in line with your trunk in the 'Y' position, palms facing front. Focus your eyes on the entry point. Move your weight forwards onto the balls of your feet, then check the movement. At this moment bend your knees and spring, driving your hips up, at the same time moving your shoulders forward. The combined movement will provide the rotation necessary

Plate 16. Spring Header position

to perform the dive. The bend at the hips is held throughout the flight up to the moment the body enters the water. Bring your hands together just prior to the entry. The angle of entry should be near to vertical but never past vertical. You will require a depth of water equal to your own height with hands reaching above head, feet pointed. You are now ready to perform the Plain Header with confidence.

The Y Position *(Fig. 29)*   This is the arm position used for the Plain Header. The arms are held above the head in line with the body, when viewed from the side, a little more than shoulder width apart. The palms face front with the fingers together.

Each of the Standing Dives (Nos. 4 to 7) should be practised first with arms in the entry position, hands clasped together as described. Each dive may then be attempted starting with the arms in the Y position. The Y position is held until just prior to the entry when the hands should be brought together.

The Pike Fall starting in the Y position should be practised from each height you intend to dive from to acquire entry control.

7. The Plain Header

For many years the English Header was taught to schoolchildren as a basic dive for use from the bathside and from firm boards up to a height of 10 feet (3 m). In this dive, the arms, from a raised position in front of and level with the shoulders, were swung downwards past the hips then upward in time with the leg spring, to a position above the head. This straight body and limb position assumed at take-off was maintained throughout the flight and entry, the forward rotation required being obtained by overbalancing during the take-off. That there was no movement of the limbs during flight made it a seemingly easy dive to perform. It did, however, prove a very difficult dive to teach to beginners from the bathside, often resulting in frustration and disappointment on the part of both teacher and pupil. Teachers often blamed themselves for the lack of results obtained, and began to regard diving as a sport strictly for the specialist.

Introduction of the Plain Header   When expert competitive divers were asked to demonstrate the English Header from the bathside, the resulting ludicrous performance was received in stunned silence. They found it virtually impossible to perform correctly. After campaigning for many years to abolish the English Header, in 1961 I introduced the Plain Header as a direct replacement. This was officially approved, and the teaching of diving to schoolchildren took a surge forward. Teachers who had experience of teaching both the English Header and the Plain Header welcomed the change as the Plain Header, which starts with the arms above the head, is much easier to teach. Also many teachers find that they themselves can now enter the water for the first time without a 'smack'.

From the teaching point of view, the Plain Header has the advantage that it follows logically from the preceding stages. There is now an element of similarity, a linking factor between the progressive practices and the finished product.

Use of the Plain Header   The Plain Header is the basic dive used in school competitions. Its use is mainly confined to the bathside or low diving boards. It can, however, be performed quite safely from any board up to the maximum height of 10 metres (33 ft). When it was first introduced it was considered a low board dive because of the danger of 'going over' on entry. This was because divers were conditioned to lean at take-off to counteract the retarding effect of the upward armswing required in the English Header. Divers brought up on the Y position take-off are not required to lean excessively, so find that the Plain Header take-off once learnt gives greater control with less chance of going over on entry.

Whereas the English Header was confined to school diving and had no transfer to more advanced diving, the Plain Header is used universally by divers at all levels. It embodies the correct techniques of diving so is a necessary step in the learning process for all dives in the Forward group. When the Plain Header has been mastered from the bathside it can be performed standing from the 1 metre springboard. It should then be performed with the one-step approach and hurdle, working up to the three-step approach. It is the basic dive in the Forward group from which progress to the pike, tuck and straight positions can easily be made.

The Value of the Plain Header The Plain Header is a 'natural' dive; it follows the normal sequence that occurs when anyone dives into the water. The straight, pike or tuck positions are not natural positions whereas the 'bent at hips' position is.

One of the common injuries with beginners occurs in the lower back through arching the back on entry. The 'bent at hips' position develops abdominal control which helps prevent accidents of this sort happening. In addition it also gives a degree of control over the rate of spin (angular velocity) during the flight. The Y position of the arms also allows additional control over the spin. If the arms are taken straight to the entry position as in the English Header there is no control available. Pupils with lack of mobility in the shoulders find it difficult to get the arms in line with the body when the arms are together. The Y position allows the arms to be back in line with the trunk.

Performing the Plain Header *(Fig. 29)* Although the whole dive is one smooth continuous sequence of movement, it is helpful to discuss it under four main headings, i.e. Starting Position, Take-off, Flight and Entry. The approach to the starting position although not judged in competition should be confident, with the body erect and under control. Focus the eyes on the take-off position on the edge, walk towards it and take up the erect position with your arms by your sides. Make sure that you are comfortable and cannot slip. Put a towel over the edge if necessary.

The Starting Position The body should be erect, feet together or just slightly apart, toes gripping the edge, and heels down (a position with the heels touching and feet apart gives good control of balance).

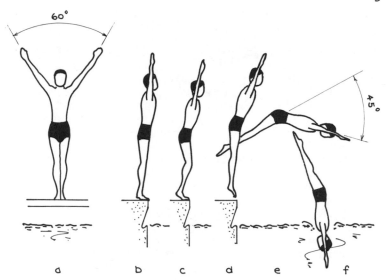

Fig. 29. The Plain Header

The arms are then raised sideways and upwards in line with the body to a position a little more than shoulder width apart, palms facing front, fingers together (the Y position). There is a pause in this position, the body remaining perfectly still and balanced.

The Take-off   The body weight is transferred slowly to the balls of the feet, causing the heels to rise slightly. The body is poised momentarily in this position, checking any tendency to overbalance at this stage. When this checkpoint is reached, the knees bend slightly and straighten quickly whilst the legs give a final vigorous push, driving the hips upward. As the feet give their final thrust, the shoulders move forward and the body bends slightly at the hips. At the moment the feet leave the side the hips should be directly above the feet. The arms should remain straight and fixed in relation to the body during the whole of the take-off movement.

The Flight   As the feet leave the side, the legs should be straight with the toes pointed. The back should be straight with no hunching of the shoulders. The body is bent forward at the hips slightly with the arms in the Y position. The bend at the hips is then increased slightly into the flight position and held until just prior to the entry. The arms remain in the Y position until just prior to the entry when they should be brought together. At the same time the bend at the hips is decreased slightly.

The Entry   As the fingers touch the water, the trunk should be as near vertical as possible, but not beyond it, with the body still bent slightly at the hips. As the trunk submerges, the body should be straightened, bringing the legs into line with the trunk. The legs should be straight at the knees, with the feet together and the toes pointed. This position should be held until the tips of the toes have disappeared under the surface, at which point the dive has been completed.

The Mechanics of the Plain Header   It is now generally recognized that the rotation (angular momentum) required in any dive must originate during the take-off, that is, whilst the feet are still in contact with the board.

In the Plain Header angular momentum is achieved by:

(1) *Overbalancing* forwards at the beginning of the take-off. Only a slight amount of rotation is obtained in this way as it is essential to keep the hips over the feet during the leg thrust in order to produce height during the flight.

A slight overbalancing is necessary to set the body in motion away from the side or board for reasons of safety. This is achieved as the shoulders move forward while the hips remain over the feet, so moving the centre of gravity in front of the feet.

(2) *Eccentric Leg Thrust*. This means moving the trunk forwards, the body bending at the hips so that the centre of gravity is in front of the hip joint as the legs push upwards (Fig. 29). This produces both upward movement of, and rotation about the centre of gravity. (Note: the greater the distance between the hip joint and the centre of gravity, the greater is the amount of angular momentum created – but less force is available to project the centre of gravity upwards and so less height is obtained and vice versa.)

(3) *Transfer of Momentum*. By moving the trunk, head, shoulders and arms in the required forward direction whilst the feet are in contact with the board, the angular momentum stored in the upper part of the body during this action will be transferred to the whole body when the feet leave the board.

The amount of momentum created will depend on the speed at which the upper body is moving as the feet leave the board. The greater the speed (angular velocity) the greater will be the angular momentum created and vice versa.

The Resulting Force   In the Plain Header there are no retarding movements. The single action of bending at the hips at take-off combined with the spring from the legs produces rotation (angular momentum) by three different methods. It also sets the centre of gravity moving away from the board, an essential requirement for safety, and also gives height to the dive.

Control of the Dive   If insufficient rotation is produced at take-off, it is necessary to pike deeper and spread the arms wider to speed up rotation, or, if too much rotation is created, the body should be straightened during flight and the arms closed earlier to reduce the rate of rotation. These movements are usually performed instinctively even by a beginner to correct a faulty take-off.

Faults and Corrections   The basic faults are, entering very short or flat, or the opposite, i.e. going over on entry. A fault that sometimes goes unnoticed is that of closing the arms together in time with the leg spring. The Y position should be held. This not only allows for some degree of control during flight, but it presents a more pleasing profile when viewed from the side. To correct this fault, the pupil should be asked to attempt to enter the water with the arms still in the Y position. When this can be achieved, he is then asked to hold the position for as long as possible and close the arms just before the entry.

Entering very short, and too far away from the side is due to insufficient rotation imparted to the body, caused by excessive lean on take-off. Too much lean limits the amount of rotation to that obtained by overbalancing at take-off. Height is also reduced by excessive lean and therefore the diver has less time in which to perform his dive.

To correct this fault, return to the previous practice of the Spring Header (Fig. 28). This will encourage greater proficiency at driving the hips up to create rotation.

If there is still a tendency to lean forward, try pushing the hips back when springing. Gradually straighten the body at each practice until it is possible to enter vertically from the starting position for the Plain Header.

Make sure to 'check' the overbalancing just before the spring, pulling the abdomen in, and moving the shoulders forward quickly. Remember to push vigorously with the feet, pointing the toes at take-off. The feeling should be one of standing on tiptoe.

The fault of entering short should not be confused with the well known 'Belly Flop' caused usually through fear.

Going over on entry coupled with a hollow back is due to too much rotation imparted to the body caused by jerking the head and shoulders forward and downward at take-off. If the progressive practices have been performed correctly this fault should not develop. However, if the English Header has been learnt previously, it may be found that on trying the Plain Header, rotation will be created so easily that the body will overthrow. This fault occurs because, by jerking the head and shoulders forward and downward quickly, a great amount of momentum can be stored in the upper trunk causing excessive rotation of the body after the feet have left the side. This, combined with the rotation caused by the eccentric leg thrust in the spring will cause the body to overthrow.

To correct this, start as for the Plain Header with arms above the head and spring upward, entering the water feet first. This jump requires no rotation at all. Practise until the entry is no more than 2 feet (0.60 m) from the side. This should prevent further trouble with 'going over'. Advice to keep the eyes focused on some point at head level until after the feet have left the side will often cure this fault without recourse to the jump.

Judging Notes   Judging the English Header presented its own problems as no two persons performed it alike with very few, if any, performing it according to the conditions laid down. The Plain Header being performed more easily by the average schoolchild results in a higher general level of skill. When judging the Plain Header the following points should be borne in mind.

Marks should be awarded from 0 to 10, in increments of half points, and the dive judged as a whole, not divided into parts for separate marking. The judge should look for the following main features:

(1) That reasonable height is obtained at take-off.

(2) That a smooth flight is achieved without undulations or excessive bend at the hips.

(3) That the entry is near to, but does not exceed, the vertical.

8. *The Basic Forward Dives*

When the Plain Header has been mastered the question poses itself, 'Where do we go from here; what dive should we learn next?' The following dives are suggested as well within the learning ability of the average schoolchild. They include the Forward Dives in the pike and tuck positions, the Forward Somersault and the Sitting Dives.

These dives can all be learnt from the side of the bath, then taken to the 1 metre springboard or firmboard, whichever is available.

THE FORWARD PIKE AND TUCK

1. Open Pike Dive *(Fig. 30)*   The starting position and take-off are as for the Plain Header. The only difference is in the flight position. The bend at the hips is increased to 90° and the arms are lowered sideways to a horizontal position. This is a natural progression from the Plain Header and the same faults and corrections apply.

Fig. 30. Open Pike Dive

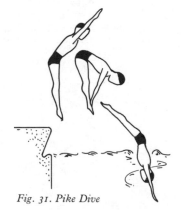

Fig. 31. Pike Dive

2. Pike Dive *(Fig. 31)*   This follows on from the Open Pike dive. The bend at the hips is increased and the arms are carried downwards for the hands to touch the ankles before opening out for the entry. As the feet leave the side they should move *forward* in front of the hips. The feeling is one of moving the feet forward towards the hands, not the hands reaching back to touch the feet.

This is not an easy dive to perform from the bathside. It is much easier to do from the 1 metre board because of the extra time available. The head must be kept up at take-off to prevent excessive rotation. If difficulty is found in preventing excessive rotation, then the Pike Jump which has no rotation may correct this.

3. Pike Jump   The take-off is as for a plain jump. *After* the feet leave the side, the body bends at the hips, the legs rising forward to a near horizontal position. The hands touch the ankles before straightening for the feet-first entry.

4. Tuck Dive *(Fig. 32)*   The mechanics of the take-off are identical with that of the Pike Dive. When in the tuck position, however, the body rotates faster than it does in the pike position, so less turn is needed at take-off. In practice, this means that the take-off is more upright, the head is kept up and the shoulders are not moved forwards so far.

As the feet leave the bathside the knees are drawn up in front of the body, and the hands move downwards to clasp the legs below the knees. The back must be rounded and the head kept up. The body rotates until the hips are higher than the head before opening out.

A common fault is to open out into a hollow-back position. This must be avoided at all costs, as it will be impossible to obtain a vertical entry from a hollow-back position. The entry should be made in a slight pike position.

Fig. 32. Tuck Dive

5. Tuck Jump   The Tuck Jump is used as a corrective exercise to prevent excessive rotation in the Tuck Dive. The tuck position with a *rounded* back and knees well up should be shown briefly before straightening for the feet-first entry.

THE FORWARD SOMERSAULT

The Forward Somersault from the bathside needs maximum force at take-off for it to be successful. It is not possible to lead into it gradually, it needs courage. However, the following progressions starting in the water will break down many of the inhibitions that prevent a whole-hearted attempt being made.

6. Glide and Somersault *(Fig. 33)*   Starting in the water from a push and glide, the head is immediately ducked under as the legs bend at the knees into a tuck position. The arms should be extended sideways to balance the body as the head submerges.

The body will rotate forwards to the head-up position.

Fig. 33. Glide and Somersault

7. Crouch Spring Somersault *(Fig. 34)*   Starting in a crouch position *standing* in water chest deep, the head and shoulders are jerked forward as the hips are pushed up. The legs bend at the knees as the body somersaults forward in the water until the feet can be placed on the bottom.

Fig. 34. Crouch Spring Somersault

8. Sitting Somersault *(Fig. 35)*   From a sitting position on the side with the feet on the rail or trough, the same movements as in Crouch

Spring Somersault (Fig. 34) are performed trying to rotate as far round as possible before entering the water.

Fig. 35. Sitting Somersault   Fig. 36. Tuck Roll

9. Tuck Roll *(Fig. 36)*   Starting on the side in a tuck position, sitting on the heels with the toes gripping the edge, the hands are placed behind for support. The body overbalances forward, the hands clasping the legs below the knees, and the head is held down. The entry is usually on the shoulders.

10. Dive and Roll *(Fig. 37)*   Starting in any comfortable standing position with the arms above the head, a normal dive entry is performed. As the trunk submerges, the chin is tucked in and the body bends at the hips and knees, and somersaults forward below the surface.

As confidence is gained, the somersault is started earlier and earlier until the body is tucked as the finger-tips touch the water. This exercise is invaluable for the beginner with little natural ability, being the closest he may get to performing a somersault.

Fig. 37. Dive and Roll

11. Crouch Somersault Starting in a comfortable crouch position with the hands above the head, a spring is made driving the hips upwards as the head, shoulders and arms are 'jerked' forward. Directly the feet leave the side, the knees are drawn up into a tuck position to speed up the rotation of the body. After one somersault the legs are straightened for the feet-first entry. Whether or not a somersault has been performed will depend on the head position at entry. If the head rotates under the body without touching the water, i.e. the back touches first, then a somersault has been performed, albeit a poor one.

12. Standing Somersault *(Fig. 38)* Starting with the body erect, arms stretched above the head, the knees bend slightly and the legs straighten quickly. The remainder of the take-off is identical to that of the Crouch Somersault. The extra height in the starting position allows more time in which to complete the rotation and stretch the legs for the entry. The aim should be for a tight tuck position with the hands clasping the shins to ensure a fast somersault.

Fig. 38. Standing Somersault

13. Running Somersault A forward somersault from the bathside is easier to perform with a run than from a standing take-off. To prevent slipping, a towel should be placed over the edge of the bath. It is advisable to practise first using the 'one step and hop' approach.

Running Firmboard Take-off

1. Starting with the feet together, a step forward is taken followed by a low hop from the same foot, to land with both feet together. Practise to find which is the best foot to hop from.

2. This is repeated two paces back from the bath edge to land near the edge in a crouch position, hands above the head.

3. Repeat, and perform the somersault into the water.

Arm Position at Take-off   To avoid excessive rotation when performing running 'headers' from the bathside, the arms should swing upwards from *the hips* at take-off. To obtain the necessary rotation required for somersaults, however, the arms should always start from a position *above the head* at the take-off.

SITTING DIVES

The Sitting Dives often provide an easy introduction to entering head first from the higher boards, as well as an introduction to the Forward $1\frac{1}{2}$ Somersaults. The Sitting Dive is also used by the expert to perfect his entries from the higher boards.

14. Basic Sitting Dive   The pupil sits on the end of the board with the hands gripping the front edge. He then leans forward and topples over into the water. The pupil should be encouraged to hold on to the board for as long as possible, then push away.

Plate 17. Sitting Dive, 3 metre springboard

15. Sitting Tuck Dive *(Fig. 39)*   Starting by sitting in a tuck position as near as possible to the front edge, with the hands gripping the end of the board either side of the hips.

The body overbalances slowly until the head is below the level of the board. A push is given with the hands and the body stretches for the entry.

Fig. 39. Sitting Tuck Dive   *Fig. 40. Sitting Pike Dive*

16. Sitting Pike Dive *(Fig. 40)*   Starting by sitting in a pike position *back* from the edge, hands gripping the end of the board either side of the knees. The hips are raised and the shoulders move forward taking the weight on the arms. The body overbalances slowly, the hands push away and the body straightens for the entry. The hands grip the edge for as long as possible to control the speed of the overbalancing at take-off.

The eyes spot the entry from start to finish; the head is kept up.

Advanced Sitting Dives   When the sitting dives in the tuck and pike positions can be performed well consistently, the hands should be released from the board immediately the body commences to overbalance.

The hands grasp the front of the legs just below the knees for the tuck position. For the pike position, the hands grip the backs of the legs below the knees. These two skills provide an introduction to the Forward $1\frac{1}{2}$ Somersaults.

9 Back Dives for Beginners

The Back Dive is a much more advanced skill than the Plain Header. Provided that it is tackled in the right way, however, it is a dive that is well within the reach of most divers.

It is a 'blind dive' because it is not possible to see where the body is going. If a diver has any fear of going backwards this must be overcome before a successful attempt can be made to perform the dive from the bathside. The fear of going backwards is a natural one, but if the body is allowed to get used to the idea gradually, it will very soon adapt itself to what at first was an unnatural movement.

Essential Features
I. When performing Back Dives from the bathside, the body *must be allowed to overbalance backwards for safety* before the spring is made. In this way there is no danger of striking the side.
II. The eyes should be focused on some object at the start and during the take-off to stabilize the body.
III. The head *must* be kept pressed back throughout the flight and the entry.

WATER PRACTICES

The following three exercises, which can be practised in shallow water, will prove invaluable in breaking down the natural fear mechanism present when falling backwards. Some pupils are able to overcome this fear very quickly and will have no difficulty in throwing the head back at the first attempt. Others may need many attempts before the head can be put back with confidence.

1. Back Dive – Pushing Off from the Side *(Fig. 41)* Starting in water at least chest-deep with a back glide, the head is pressed back and the body is arched. The hands reach for the bottom, the eyes should be

Fig. 41. Back Dive, pushing off from the side

open. The pupil should progress no farther until he can press his head back beneath the surface with confidence.

2. Back Dive – Pushing Off from the Bottom *(Fig. 42)* Standing in chest-deep water with the arms above the head in the Y position, a spring backwards is made with the back arched and head back, into a back glide on the surface.

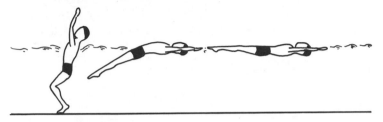

Fig. 42. Back Dive, pushing off from the bottom

3. Back Dive to Balance on Hands *(Fig. 43)* Standing in chest-deep water, the same movement as in Fig. 42 is performed except that the body arches back so that the hands can be placed on the bottom. Practise until the body can be balanced on the hands.

Fig. 43. Back Dive, to balance on hands

BATHSIDE PRACTICES

The transition from the water to the bathside is a critical one. If the Back Dive to balance on the hands (Fig. 43) can be performed with confidence then the transition will present no problems. Where there is a natural timidity, then it is advisable to progress slowly, allowing plenty of opportunity to overcome the fear of putting the head back.

In instances of this nature the Back Rolls (Figs. 44 and 47) provide an easy introduction to the dives, and it should be left to the pupil to decide when to change the 'roll' into the 'dive'.

Back Jumps for Confidence and Correction   It is good practice
to let divers get used to jumping in backwards and entering backwards
by a variety of different ways before asking them to dive in backwards
head first. These activities should be quite informal, but later the jumps
can be used with the required armswing as a corrective practice to
prevent excessive lean and excessive rotation. The back jump is
especially useful on the 1 metre springboard.

4. Back Roll from Rail *(Fig. 44)*   Starting by standing on the rail
or trough with the hands resting on the side, the body overbalances
backwards. The object is to keep the hands on the side and the feet on
the rail for as long as possible. The head is kept *forward* until the body
submerges. When this can be performed with confidence, the body
should be stretched into an arched position directly the head is
submerged.

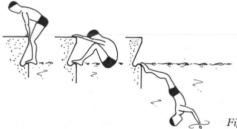

Fig. 44. Back Roll from the rail

5. Back Dive from Rail *(Fig. 45)*   Starting by standing on the rail or
trough, with the hands resting on the side, the body overbalances backwards. Almost at the same time the arms are swung backwards over the
head, as the head and shoulders are jerked backwards towards the water
in time with a spring from the legs.

Fig. 45. Back Dive from the rail

Fig. 46. Back Dive, Bent Knee

6. Back Dive, Bent Knee *(Fig. 46)* Starting with one foot on the rail and the other on the edge of the bath, hands above the head, the body overbalances backwards. The arms, head and shoulders are then jerked backwards in time with a spring from the bent knee so that the body enters backwards head first. As a preparatory exercise this can be performed as a jump with a feet-first entry, to give the pupils the opportunity to get used to the bent-knee take-off.

Plate 18. Back Dive Bent Knee position   Plate 19. Back Tuck Roll position

7. Back Tuck Roll *(Fig. 47)*   Starting in a tuck position sitting on the heels, back to the water with the fingers resting on the deck, the body overbalances backwards. The fingers drag along the side and maintain contact with the side for as long as possible. The head is kept forward. The hands grasp the shins and the body rolls back into the water in a tight tuck position.

Fig. 47. Back Tuck Roll

8. Back Tuck Roll with Stretch *(Fig. 47)*   The previous exercise is repeated but directly the head is submerged, the back is arched and the diver circles up to the surface near to the side.

9. Back Tuck Roll Dive *(Fig. 48)*   Starting in a tuck position sitting on the heels, back to the water with the fingers resting on the deck, the body overbalances backwards. Almost immediately the arms are thrown over the head towards the water as the body arches and the legs extend vigorously to get the body in head first.

Plate 20. Back Tuck Roll Dive

Plate 21. Back Tuck Roll Dive

Fig. 48. Back Tuck Roll Dive   *Fig. 49. Back Crouch Dive*

10. Back Crouch Dives *(Fig. 49)*   Starting in any comfortable standing position with the back to the water and the heels projecting over the edge, the body overbalances backwards. Just as the balance is lost, but before the body falls too far, the arms are swung upwards and backwards with the back arching and the legs extending for the spring. The eyes look for the water and the entry is made hands first followed by the head. Depending on the pupil's confidence, the Back Crouch Dive can progress from a very low crouch position to a high crouch position, through as many intermediate stages as the pupil feels necessary.

Use of the Armswing   By swinging the arms upwards and backwards, momentum will be stored in them which will assist the backward rotation of the body as a whole. In the early stages of learning, when the main object is to get in somehow, this can be of great assistance. As confidence develops the rotation created by the armswing may become a hindrance to the correct performance of the dive by creating excessive rotation at the expense of height. This can be prevented by using rotation, created by the head and shoulders rather than relying on the armswing. By this method a Back Dive can be performed with the minimum amount of lean.

11. Back Spring Header   Starting in the erect position with the arms above the head (Y position), the body overbalances backwards. Just as the balance is lost, the legs bend at the knees slightly and then straighten quickly. As the spring is made the head and shoulders jerk backwards, the back is arched and the eyes look back for the water. The angle of take-off should be such that the feet rise vertically above the bath edge until the body is horizontal. The entry should not be too far out and should not exceed the height of the body. The arms should remain in the Y position until just prior to the entry. A common fault is leaning back too far before the spring is made.

SPRINGBOARD PRACTICES

12. Back Fall – 1 metre   A Back Dive from the 1 metre springboard is very easy *physically*. It is only the mental (fear) barrier that has to be overcome. The danger is that of excessive rotation resulting in a painful smack on the legs.

Starting from the Y position the body overbalances *slowly*. The body arches and the eyes look back for the water. There must be no spring – just a back fall into the water.

13. Back Tuck Roll Dive – 1 metre   Natural timidity may prevent some divers from attempting the Back Fall from the 1 metre board. They may find a Back Tuck Roll Dive (Fig. 48) an easier approach. This can be performed quite safely and the lack of height will lessen the force of impact.

14. Back Dives – 1 metre   When the Back Fall can be performed consistently, the Back Spring Header may be attempted. It should be performed very slowly at first to prevent excessive rotation. The eyes should focus on the back end of the board during the take-off. The armswing should be introduced by means of a back jump, then performed *slowly* into a back dive. The arms should reach *up* rather than back, as if trying to lift off the board.

Observations   In the early stages of learning the Back Dive the body should overbalance first, followed by the spring to ensure sufficient clearance. In later stages, especially from the springboards, the over-balancing takes place as the diver extends his legs in the spring. He should still be in balance on the board during the crouch.

10. *Inward, Twist and Reverse Dives*

The dives covered in this chapter represent the more difficult groups: the Inward Twist and Reverse. The Reverse and Inward are 'scarey' dives with a great deal of fear to be overcome by most pupils, especially with the Reverse group. The Twist group is quite safe, but difficult because of its complexity. These dives present problems not only to the pupil but also to the inexperienced teacher, who may not feel qualified to teach them through ignorance of what is required.

By working slowly through the graduated practices suggested, both teacher and pupil will gain a greater understanding of the essentials of these more difficult dives. The Inward Dive should be tackled first, followed by the Twist Dives. It is advisable to leave the Reverse Dives to those with an above average ability, although the 'work ups' can be performed by all.

The greatest danger is the *inconsistency* usually present in beginners with average or less than average ability.

INWARD DIVES

The dives in this group are in effect Forward Dives performed from a back take-off so the equivalent Forward Dive is a necessary prerequisite in the learning programme. The pupil must also be quite confident at jumping in backwards. This should be achieved when learning the Back Dives.

Essential Features
I. When performing Inward Dives from the bathside it is essential that enough *clearance* is obtained at take-off. With beginners, this is achieved by *leaning backwards* before the spring is made.
II. During the learning stages the hands should be in a position above the head at take-off and during the flight, for protection.
III. The eyes should be focused on some fixed object to stabilize the body at the start and during the take-off.
IV. The eyes should refocus on the edge of the bath or board immediately the feet lose contact.

1. Inward Jump *(Fig. 50)*   Starting in the Y position a jump backwards is made, to enter the water at a slight forward angle with the arms above the head. This slight inward rotation is achieved by jerking the shoulders forward as the body overbalances backwards at the take-off. No further progress should be attempted until the inward jump can be performed entering the water at an angle of 30° from the vertical.

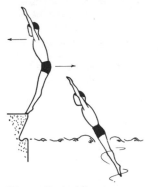

Fig. 50. *Inward Jump*   Fig. 51. *Inward Pike Drop*

2. Inward Pike Drop *(Fig. 51)*   The take-off is the same as for the Inward Jump. After the feet leave the side, the body bends at the hips with the head pressed down and the hands clasp the legs behind the knees. The entry is feet first in a pike position. This should be practised first away from the bath edge to ensure that the piking takes place *before* the feet touch the floor again. A common fault is to jump back, and then bend *after* the feet retouch the floor.

3. Inward Dive *(Fig. 52)*   The take-off is the same as for the Inward Pike Drop. After the feet leave the side, the legs are bent at the knees and the hands reach for the water, i.e. 'Try to get your hands in before your feet.' A common fault at this stage is excessive backward lean before

Fig. 52. *Inward Dive*

take-off. To correct this, keep the shoulders forward and let the hips go back, i.e. a slight pike position at take-off.

4. Inward Dive Tuck – 1 metre   Directly the Inward Dive is achieved from the bathside it should be taken to the 1 metre springboard. The extra height of the starting position and the 'lift' obtained from the board make it much easier to perform. The aim then is to clasp the shins and pull into a tight tuck position during the flight. A common fault at this stage is excessive rotation. This can be corrected by keeping the head up throughout the dive and focusing the eyes on the edge of the board. The next stage is to incorporate the armswing.

TWIST DIVES

Twist dives are confusing at first attempts because of the complication of combining 'twist' rotation about the body's long axis with somersaulting about the lateral axis. The two basic dives are the Forward Dive with Half Twist and the Back Dive with Half Twist. The Back Dive Half Twist is well within the scope of the average schoolchild to attempt. The Forward Half Twist may prove a more difficult nut to crack, but as there is no fear problem it is just a matter of practice. These two Twist Dives should be practised first in the water to acquire the feel of the twist rotation before attempting them from the bathside.

1. Back Glide Half Twist   From a Back *Glide*, the head is pressed back and the body rolled sideways into a slight front pike position gliding towards the bottom as after a Forward Dive entry.

2. Back Spring Half Twist   Standing in waist-deep water with the arms in the Y position, a spring backwards is made. At the same time the shoulders are twisted so that the body finishes on the front. Later this can be followed by bending at the hips to touch the bottom as in Exercise 1 above.

Fig. 53. Back Dive, Half Twist

3. Back Dive Half Twist *(Fig. 53)*   The starting position and take-off from the bathside are identical with those for the Back Spring Header (Chapter 9). As the spring is made the shoulders are twisted to either the left or the right so that the body enters as for the Plain Header. The technique required is an arched back at take-off, twisting into a slight pike position for the entry.

4. Front Glide Half Twist   From a Front Glide *below* the surface, the body rolls sideways, the head is pressed back and the body arched finishing as from a Back Dive entry.

5. Front Spring Half Twist   Standing in waist-deep water with the arms in the Y position, a spring forwards is made. At the same time the shoulders are twisted so that the body finishes on the back. Later this can be followed by arching back to touch the bottom.

6. Forward Dive Half Twist   The starting position and take-off from the bathside are identical with the Spring Header (Chapter 6). As the spring is made a quarter twist is attempted aiming to enter sideways. One arm turns towards the water, the eyes looking along the arm towards the entry point. The other arm points towards the roof. The body is in a side arch position. It is better to aim for a quarter twist which will usually result in a half twist, rather than aim for a half twist which usually results in a full twist. The arms remain apart for as long as possible to ensure an arched back, closing only for the entry (see Fig. 72).

Side Take-off for Forward Twists   By taking off from a starting position standing sideways on, it is only necessary to perform a quarter twist to enter backwards. This is in effect the last half of the Forward Dive Half Twist and is for some pupils an easier approach.

Twist Technique   The correct technique is to push the hips *forward* arching the body when in the side arch position. The head should be pressed back. Some pupils have a 'blind' spot where twists are concerned whilst others need only one or two attempts in order to consolidate the movement. When the half twist can be performed consistently from the bathside it can be taken from the 1 metre springboard. First attempts should be from a standing take-off, arms in the Y position, then from the one step and hurdle approach with the normal armswing. The twist is taken from the board and it is sufficient just to turn the shoulders *slightly* during the rise of the board at the completion of the spring.

REVERSE DIVES

The dives in this group are in effect Back Dives performed from a forward take-off, so the equivalent Back Dive is a necessary prerequisite in the learning programme. These dives are difficult because not only are they 'blind' dives, but also the head is rotating backwards towards the board. It is very important that the teacher has a very clear understanding of the mechanics of the take-off and is able to convey this to the pupil confidently.

Essential Features

I. When performing reverse movements from the bathside it is essential that enough *clearance* is obtained at take-off (see Chapter 17). With beginners this is achieved by *leaning forwards* before the spring is made.
II. It is essential that the pupil demonstrates his ability to create reverse rotation satisfactorily in the reverse jumps, before progressing to the head-first entry.

1. Reverse Jump *(Fig. 54)*   Starting in a slight crouch position facing the water, toes gripping the edge of the bath, the body overbalances *slowly*. The arms swing from behind the hips forward and upward as a spring is made. The shoulders move back as the hips are pushed forward and the legs swing out towards the water. The body enters the water feet first at an angle of 30° from the vertical with the hands above the head in the Y position, head forward, eyes spotting the entry point (Position a). The feeling is of jumping up to catch a bar in front, then letting the legs swing forward beneath it.

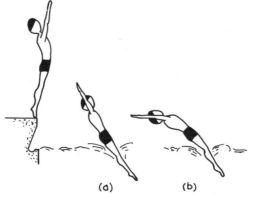

(a)   (b)   *Fig. 54. Reverse Jump*

2. Reverse Jump Arched *(Fig. 54)*   This is identical with the Reverse Jump except that the body is arched and the head is held back, eyes spotting a point on the 'ceiling'. The body enters feet first in an arched position (Position b). This is more difficult, but introduces the diver to the 'blind' part of the dive.

It is very important that the diver is able to achieve this arched position because no matter how he lands at entry he will not hurt himself while he maintains an arched back.

He should practise until he is landing nearly on to his back.

3. Reverse Dive *(Fig. 55)*   The take off is the same as for the Arched Jump but performed with more vigour. The shoulders are jerked back as the arms swing forward vigorously to create the extra rotation needed to get in head first. To speed up the rotation the legs should be bent at the knees and the arms taken out sideways. The Reverse Dive should then be performed standing from the 1 metre board.

Fig. 55. Reverse Dive

4. Reverse Dive Straight – 1 metre   Directly the dive can be achieved from the 1 metre board, the Reverse Jump should be practised with a one step and hurdle approach to get the 'feel' of the take-off. When the diver feels ready he performs the one step and hurdle into the Reverse Dive. As he takes off he should push his chest forward and up, and look for a point on the ceiling immediately above the end of the board.

If there is no springboard available or the two-foot take-off presents problems, the *one-foot* firmboard take-off technique can be used as follows.

5. Reverse Kick Jump *(Fig. 56)*   Starting with one foot on the edge and the other foot back from the edge, the arms are swung forward from behind the hips, in time with a kick forward and upward from the rear leg. The body enters the water foot first, at an angle of 30° from the vertical with the kicking leg in the air and the arms in the Y position, with the head forward and eyes spotting the entry (Position a).

(a)   (b)

Fig. 56. Reverse Kick Jump

6. Reverse Kick Jump Arched *(Fig. 56)*   The same procedure is then followed as with the Reverse Jump. The Kick Jump is repeated with an arched back to get the feel of the 'blind' part of the dive (Position b). It should then be performed from the 'one step and kick' take-off (see Exercise 8).

7. Reverse Kick Dive *(Fig. 57)*   The take-off is as for the Reverse Kick Jump Arched, but performed with more vigour, aiming to enter head first. It can be tried from the standing one foot take-off or from the one step and kick take-off.

Fig. 57. Reverse Kick Dive

8. One Step and Kick (*Firmbound Take-off*)   For the one step and kick take-off, a position one pace back is taken up with the feet together. All that is required is a step forward on to the edge of the bath followed by the kick from the rear leg. It is advisable to place a towel over the edge to prevent slipping. The momentum from the step forward is added to that of the kick, giving greater height and more time in which to rotate sufficiently to get the head in easily.

Reverse Dives are very difficult to perform from the bathside unless the diver has a supple back to enable his head to enter easily. If a low firmboard is available the one step and kick take-off into a Reverse Dive is much easier to perform. When this take-off is used on the 1 metre springboard the fulcrum should be moved as far forward as possible to make the board firmer. When the one step take-off is mastered, additional steps can be added, but should be performed *slowly* to avoid 'skating' off the board at take-off.

11. *Using the Springboard*

The springboard is a device used to obtain additional *height* from the take-off. It is important to stress this basic fact to all divers when starting springboard diving.

The mechanical principles involved in obtaining height are discussed fully in Chapter 16 and the other requirements of the take-off are dealt with in Chapters 17 and 18.

THE RUNNING TAKE-OFF (*Fig. 58*)

The word 'run' is misleading. The running take-off from the springboard consists of a three-step *walk* followed by a jump upwards from one foot to land on the end of the board with both feet at the same time. In a running dive from the springboard, the diver must take at least four steps in all, including the take-off from the end of the board, which must

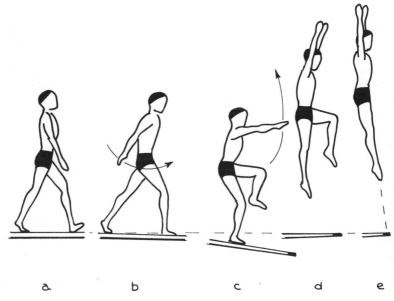

a   b   c   d   e

Fig. 58. The Running Take-off

be from both feet simultaneously. From the springboard, all Forward and Reverse Dives with or without Twist should preferably be performed from a running take-off. It may be an advantage to perform a standing forward take-off occasionally as a beginner, but the running forward approach should be performed whenever possible. For the purpose of description, the running take-off can be divided into five parts:

1. The walk (a minimum of three steps)
2. The hurdle (the jump upwards from one foot)
3. The crouch (the soft landing on the end of the board)
4. The drive down (the depressing of the board)
5. The push up (the acceleration of the body upwards during the recoil)

1. The Walk   The first two steps of the approach are normal walking steps (Fig. 58a), but the third step is slightly longer and faster. There is a gradual acceleration and a gathering of effort. On the third step, which is from 2 to 3 feet from the end of the board, the knee of the leading leg will bend more to provide the spring for the hurdle (Fig. 58b). The body weight will depress the board.

f   g   h   i   j

A common fault is leaning back during the walk. The weight should be forward, shoulders over the leading foot. The body should be erect with the abdominals contracted (stomach pulled in).

2. The Hurdle As the body moves forward over the take-off leg, the knee begins to straighten depressing the board still farther. From a position behind the hips, the arms swing forwards and upwards; at the same time the knee of the rear leg is raised forwards and upwards level with the hip, the lower leg being at 90° to the thigh. This combined action further depresses the board (Fig. 58c). As the board recoils upwards the arms rise to a Y position above the head, the take-off leg straightens and the heel is raised as the foot pushes against the rising board, accelerating the body upwards into the hurdle (Fig. 58d). At the peak of the hurdle the bent knee starts to straighten and the rear leg moves forward, but the arms remain in a balanced Y position at either side of the head. The eyes which have been focused on the tip of the board from the commencement of the run, continue to watch it as the body descends, the head being kept as erect as possible (Fig. 58e).

The hurdle should be a well-controlled easy rise from the board. A common fault is putting too much effort into the hurdle and reaching up too high causing the shoulder girdle to rise (hunching). The shoulders should be kept down in their normal position. The maximum reaction to the armswing occurs when the arms are horizontal, at which point the board is nearing maximum deflection (Fig. 58c). As the board recoils, projecting the body upwards, the arms, which are now at head level having done their work, 'float' into the Y position (Fig. 58d). Note: this 'delay' at the top of the armswing is very important in the execution of the hurdle jump.

3. The Crouch As the body descends on to the end of the board the feet are just in front of the hips. The arms start to swing down sideways and slightly backwards. Just before the feet make contact (Fig. 58f), the legs bend slightly at the knees, the ankles flex and the landing is made *softly* on the balls of the feet, the knees continue to bend until the heels make contact when the full weight of the body depresses the board. The arms moving downwards with increasing speed have reached a position just behind the hips (Fig. 58g).

4. The Drive Down As the board descends, the arms swing vigorously forwards and upwards past the hips in time with the start of a strong leg push (Fig. 58h). This combined arm and leg action, coordinated with the downward movement of the board, will drive the board down with great force. When the board reaches its lowest point the hands will be approximately at head level with the knees bent and the heels down. The

Plate 22.
Giorgio Cagnotto *(Italy)*
European Springboard
Champion 1970
(Barcelona), demon-
strates the 'Hurdle'

body should be balanced on the end of the board, the shoulders directly above the feet with no suggestion of lean (Fig. 58i).

5. The Push Up As the board recoils, accelerating the body upwards, the legs give a strong final push, straightening at the knees and ankles, with the toes thrusting into the board (Fig. 58j). This combined action, co-ordinated correctly with the upward recoil of the board, will give additional upward acceleration to the body, projecting the diver high into the flight. As the board rises the arms reach up before moving in the required direction to assist if necessary in the creation of forward or backward rotation.

Observations The aim in the springboard take-off is to deflect the board as much as possible but at the same time ensure that when it reaches the bottom of its swing the heels are down with the legs still bent slightly at the knees, ready for their final extension as the board recoils (Fig. 58i). In the firmboard take-off, the diver uses his energy in pushing *up* from the board but in the springboard take-off most of his available energy is used in *depressing* the board before pushing away from it. As the diver leaves the board his hands *must* be above head level in order to obtain reasonable height from the take-off.

Learning the Running Take-off Although a simple skill to a competent diver, the running springboard take-off is very difficult for beginners to master. To avoid wasting board time with a group of learners, the take-off should be practised first on land until the movements are mastered. No attempt should be made at first to go into too great detail. The simpler the approach, the greater the chance of success. A simple method for beginners with little natural ability is to eliminate the first two steps leaving only *one step into the hurdle*. Most beginners will be able to perform this successfully at the first attempt. Any attempt to go into technical details to achieve the correct knee and arm lift of the hurdle step is liable to cause a mental block resulting in complete frustration and inability to move at all. As the actual *movements* for the running take-off are the same for both springboard and firmboard, it is advisable to learn the easier *firmboard* take-off first from the bathside.

Step and Hop, Two-Foot Take-off 1. Practise first on land. Step forward, hop, and land with both feet at the same time. Find out which is the best leg to hop from.

2. On the bathside, two paces back from the edge. Step forward *slowly* one pace, hop, and land with both feet near the bath edge, knees bent in a crouch position, hands by hips.

3. Repeat, but this time, dive in. Practise this for consistency. This is in effect the running *firmboard* take-off.

Note: No attempt should be made to mention or obtain a high hurdle. The object is to 'go through the motions' and enter the water as simply as possible, so that the learner has something basic to work on.

From the 1 Metre Board   4. Repeat the one step and 'hurdle' on the 1 metre board landing in a low crouch *near the end*.

5. Repeat with a 'dive' in from the end. (A beginner finds it easier to dive in at this stage than to jump in.)

6. Repeat, and encourage height in the 'hurdle'; push with the foot.

7. Repeat, 'getting the knee up higher' in the hurdle.

8. Repeat, 'lifting the arms up with the knee'.

9. Practise aiming for a 'delay' at the top of the armswing.

10. Practise with a *jump* entry. This is to reduce the inevitable lean at take-off.

Note: beginners will usually find a jump entry difficult because of excessive lean. Encourage reaching up with the arms at take-off (grasping an imaginary beam!) to bring the entry nearer to the board. By standing opposite the desired entry point, the teacher provides a marker for the diver to aim for. A common fault at this stage is 'swimming through' with the arms. As the diver rises from the board he swings his arms in a quick circle, so that when he is at the peak of the jump, his arms are by his sides instead of above his head in the Y position (Fig. 58d,e).

11. To correct this, enter the water feet first with the hands above the head in the Y position.

12. Repeat, but lower the arms to the sides just prior to the entry.

13. Attempt to repeat the one step and hurdle, into a 'dive', entering at the same point as with the jump.

Note: The dive should be the basic Plain Header, i.e. the simplest method of entering head first.

The Three-step Approach   14. When the one step and hurdle can be performed consistently, include the additional two steps, i.e. one, two, three, hop, land on the end, stop. This can be practised on land first, then from the 1 metre board into the water. (Remember that the three-step approach starts with the same foot as the one step approach.) Slowly at first, landing on the board softly (as if landing on broken glass!) then *push*.

THE BACK TAKE-OFF (*Fig. 59*)

The Back Take-off is used for all Back and Inward Dives with or without Twist. This section should be read in conjunction with Chapter 16.

For the purpose of description the Back Take-off is divided into four parts:

    1. The preparatory armswing (to set the board in motion)
    2. The crouch (in preparation for the dive)
    3. The drive down (the final depressing of the board)
    4. The push up (the accelerating of the body upwards during the final recoil)

Fig. 59. The Back Take-off

1. The Preparatory Armswing From the back stance with the arms by the sides the board is set in motion downwards by raising the arms sideways (Fig. 59a) reaching shoulder height as the board reaches the bottom of its swing. As the board recoils upwards the arms continue to rise to a position just above the head level. The heels are raised, toes pressing into the board as the board approaches the top of its swing (Fig. 59b). A common fault is to allow the feet to leave the board at this point. This can be prevented by ensuring that the shoulders are kept down in their normal position. If the arms are raised too vigorously the shoulders may rise and cause a slight but undesirable loss of balance.

2. The Crouch At this moment the knees start to bend into a deep crouch, and the arms swing with increasing speed downwards, sideways and slightly backwards toward the hips. This combined action will relieve the weight on the board and it will remain still (Figs. 59c and d).

3. The Drive Down As the board starts to descend for the second time, the arms swing vigorously forwards and upwards past the hips in time with the start of a strong leg push. This combined arm and leg action, co-ordinated with the downward recoil of the board, will drive the board down with great force. When the board reaches its lowest point the hands will be approximately at head level, with the knees bent and heels down. The body should be balanced on the end of the board, the shoulders directly above the feet with no suggestion of lean (Fig. 59e).

4. The Push Up As the board recoils, accelerating the body upwards, the legs give a strong final push, straightening at the knees and ankles, with the toes thrusting into the board (Fig. 59f). The combined action, co-ordinated correctly with the upward recoil of the board, will give additional upward acceleration to the body, projecting the diver high into the flight.

As the board rises, the arms *reach up*, before moving in the required direction to assist if necessary in the creation of forward or backward rotation.

Learning the Back Take-off 1. Practise on land at first the armswing in slow motion, with a jump on the spot. Start with the arms by the sides. Raise the arms sideways slowly, at the same time raising the heels. Circle the arms down behind and bend the knees. Swing the arms forwards and upwards in time with the jump. Land with the hands above the head at first to acquire the *delay* at the top of the armswing.

2. Repeat with backward travel on land.

3. Repeat from the bathside with a back jump into the water, entering with hands above head.

4. Practise the take-off on the 1 metre springboard, starting one pace back from the end, to land back on the board.

5. Perform the back take-off from the end of the board, i.e. back jump into the water entering with the hands above the head in the Y position.

6. Repeat, but lower the arms to the sides just prior to the entry.

SUMMARY

As the board recoils and before the feet lose contact, three actions must take place:

(1) The body must be projected *upwards* with maximum velocity, to gain the *time* required to complete the dive.

(2) The body must be set in motion *away from the board* for *safety*.

(3) The body movements necessary to produce the turning force required for the creation of angular momentum must be *completed*.

This final phase of the take-off is the most important. Any fault seen during the flight and entry can usually be traced to faulty take-off technique.

The correct performance of the dive depends more on the take-off than any other factor. Errors at take-off cannot be fully corrected during the flight. The essence of a good take-off is the perfect co-ordination of the movements of the body, and limbs with the movements of the board.

12. *Basic Dives from the Springboard*

Before the basic dives are attempted from the springboard, the fundamental requirements of the take-off described in Chapters 16, 17 and 18, should be understood.

To appreciate fully the body movements required during the flight Chapter 19 ('Control of Rotation in Flight') should be read in conjunction with Chapter 14 ('Body Movement in Free Fall').

The dives are not listed in order of difficulty. The basic dive in the pike position is described first in each group because it has the most movement and is, therefore, the most suitable for purposes of description.

The diver should learn, and be able to perform consistently, each dive in all three positions.

The pike and tuck positions are necessary prerequisites for Pike and Tuck Somersaults, because the straight position has different requirements at take-off that can be detrimental to their correct execution.

FORWARD DIVE PIKE (*Fig. 60*)

The Take-off As the board recoils upwards, the trunk is erect with the hips directly over the feet. The arms reach up, the head is held erect, the abdomen is drawn in, the shoulders move forwards slightly, the body bending at the hips as the feet give their final push.

The body's centre of gravity is just forward beyond the point of support (the feet) setting the body overbalancing slowly so that it will be projected upwards and outwards with forward rotation. Angular momentum is obtained from overbalancing, eccentric leg thrust and transfer of momentum from the head and shoulders.

The Flight The body rises from the board and begins to bend slowly at the hips. As the body bends into the pike position, its resistance to rotation (moment of inertia) will decrease, and in direct consequence the rate of rotation (angular velocity) will increase. The hips rise behind the centre of gravity to a position above the level of the head, at the same time the feet move forward to a position below and slightly in front of the hips. The head and arms are kept up in line with the trunk until the hips complete their movement at the peak of the dive, at which point the hands touch the feet. The body, now in its fastest rotating position, turns as it descends, until the feet move back to a position below and slightly behind the hips. At this point the body is unpiked slowly so that

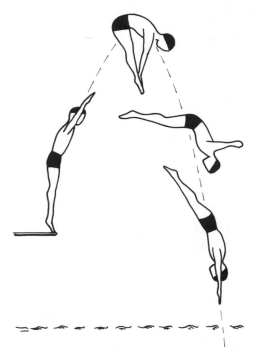

Fig. 60. Forward Dive Pike

the upper trunk keeps in position along the projected line of flight, whilst the legs rise behind until they are in line with the trunk. At the same time the arms, from their position by the feet, open out sideways, then close together above the head. The body is now rotating at its slowest rate and is a little short of vertical as the head is lowered between the outstretched arms ready for the entry.

FORWARD DIVE STRAIGHT (*Fig. 61*)

The Take-off The take-off is similar to that of the Forward Dive Pike with a slight bend at the hips just before the feet leave the board. To obtain the additional angular momentum to allow the body to rotate in the slower straight position, the shoulders are 'jerked' forward *faster*.

The Flight As the feet leave the board, the body is immediately straightened at the hips whereas in the Forward Dive Pike the body

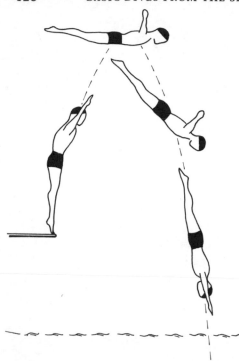

Fig. 61. Forward Dive
Straight

bends more at the hips. The arms, from the overhead position, are
taken directly out to the sides at right angles to the body. At the peak of
the dive the body should be horizontal. The body remains in the same
position throughout the dive until just prior to entry. The eyes spot the
water and the arms are brought together overhead.

FORWARD DIVE TUCK (*Fig. 62*)

The Take-off   The take-off is similar to that of the Forward Dive Pike.
To allow for the faster rotation when in the tuck position, the angular
momentum is reduced by reaching well up with the arms, and moving
the shoulders forward more slowly. The head is kept up.

The Flight   Directly the feet leave the board the legs bend at the knees
and the tuck position is assumed. To allow for the increase in angular
velocity when the tuck position is assumed, the knees should be higher

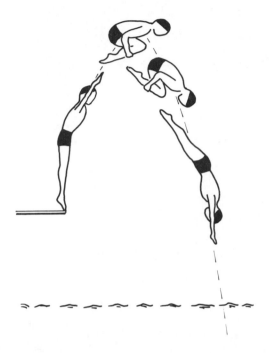

Fig. 62. Forward Dive
Tuck

than the hips. The head is held up throughout, and should be level with the hips at the peak of the dive. The legs straighten into a slight pike position prior to entry.

BACK DIVE PIKE (*Fig. 63*)

The Take-off   As the board recoils upwards the shoulders are vertically above the feet, with the hips back beyond the front end of the board. As the feet give their final push, the abdomen is drawn in and the shoulders moved back to a position above the hips. This action will move the body's centre of gravity back beyond the point of support (the balls of the feet) setting the body overbalancing slowly so that it will be projected upwards and outwards with backward rotation. The moving of the shoulders backwards will enable momentum to be stored in the upper trunk which will be transferred to the whole of the body to provide additional backward rotation when the feet leave the board. The

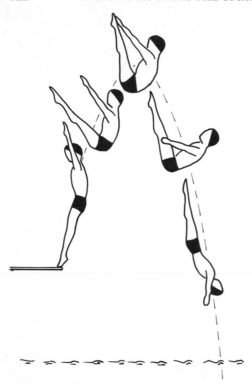

Fig. 63. Back Dive Pike

head is held erect, the hands reach up to a position in front of and above the head. (A common fault is to swing the arms back behind the head causing the shoulders to jerk back with the result that too much rotation is imparted to the body.) The feeling is one of jumping straight up. Throughout the movement the abdomen should be kept firm (there must be no arch in the back); the whole body is stretched as the feet leave the board.

The Flight At the moment the stretched body rises from the board it will be rotating about its centre of gravity at its slowest rate. Directly the feet leave the board, the body begins to bend at the hips. If performed correctly, this action, combined with the backward rotation of the body as a whole, will cause the upper trunk to remain in the same place in relation to the vertical and the legs to rise up, until the body is in the required pike position with the feet above the level of the head.

The head and arms are kept up in line with the trunk until the bending at the hips is completed, at which point the hands touch the feet at the peak of the dive.

As the legs rise into the pike position, the body's resistance to rotation (moment of inertia) will decrease, and in direct consequence the rate of rotation (angular velocity) will increase, i.e. the body spins faster. When the body is in the finished pike position it will be rotating at its fastest.

The body, descending, rotates backward in this position until the legs are in line with the projected line of flight, i.e. slightly short of vertical. At this point, the body is unpiked at such a rate that, combined with the continued backward rotation of the body as a whole, the legs remain in line with the flight curve whilst the trunk 'lowers' back until it is in line with the legs along the line of flight. As the trunk is moved back, the arms are taken sideways and upwards to a stretched position in line with the trunk above the head. The stretched body is now once more rotating at its slowest rate and is a little short of vertical as the arms reach back above the head ready for entry.

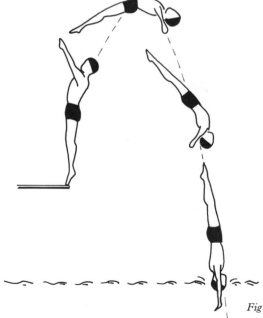

Fig. 64. Back Dive Straight

BACK DIVE STRAIGHT (*Fig. 64*)

The Take-off   As the board recoils upwards, the shoulders are vertically above the feet, with the hips back beyond the end of the board.
When the feet give their final push the shoulders are moved back from
the forward bend position to an arched position, and the hips move
forwards over the feet. This trunk action will move the body's centre of
gravity back beyond the point of support (the feet) setting the body
overbalancing slowly so that it will be projected upwards and outwards
with backward rotation. The backward movement of the shoulders will
enable the momentum stored in them to be transferred to the body when
the feet leave the board. The arms reach up above the head which is
kept in line with the trunk.

Plate 23. Carrie Irish *(U.S.A.) A.A.U. Outdoor Springboard Champion 1973:
Back Dive Straight*

The Flight   As the feet leave the board the arms are taken directly out
to the side. The eyes refocus on a point in front of and above head level.
As the body rotates to the peak of the dive it is near horizontal, the back
arches more and the head is pressed back with the eyes looking for the
water. The body remains in this position until just prior to entry. The

eyes spot the water, the arms are brought together overhead, and the trunk is straightened.

BACK DIVE TUCK (*Fig. 65*)

The Take-off   The take-off is similar to that of the Back Dive Pike. To allow for the faster rotation when in the tuck position, the angular momentum at take-off is reduced by moving the shoulders back more slowly during the final leg push.

The Flight   Directly the feet leave the board the knees are drawn up to the chest. The trunk is just past the vertical with the head forward and the knees and shoulders on the same level. The position is held, and the hips should be level with the shoulders at the peak of the dive. As the body starts to descend the legs are extended into a slight pike position, and the arms taken out directly sideways. The head is pressed back, eyes looking for the entry, and the arms are brought together overhead.

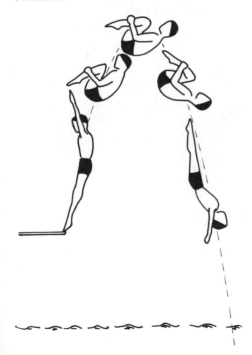

Fig. 65. Back Dive Tuck

REVERSE DIVE PIKE (*Fig. 66*)

The Take-off   As the board recoils upwards, the hands reach up, the
head is held erect, the abdomen is drawn in, the shoulders are pressed
back and the chest pushed upwards. As the feet give their final push, the
shoulders should be directly over the feet, with the upper back arched
and the hips just a little forward of the feet, placing the body's centre of
gravity forward beyond the point of support (the feet) so that it will be
projected upward and outward. The moving of the head and shoulders
backwards will enable momentum to be stored in the upper trunk which
will be transferred to the whole of the body to provide reverse rotation
when the feet leave the board.

The Flight   As far as the diver is concerned, once he has left the board
the movements required are identical to those of the Back Dive Pike
(Fig. 63). The fact that in the Reverse Dive Pike he is moving forwards

*Fig. 66. Reverse Dive
Pike*

away from the board, and in the Back Dive Pike he is moving backwards away from the board, does not affect the rotation about the centre of gravity. The horizontal component of the flight can be ignored. The description of the flight for the Back Dive Pike therefore, may be read in conjunction with the diagram for the Reverse Dive Pike.

REVERSE DIVE STRAIGHT (*Fig. 67*)

The Take-off   The take-off is similar to that of the Reverse Dive Pike. To obtain the additional angular momentum to allow the body to rotate in the slower straight position, the shoulders are 'jerked' backwards faster.

The Flight   As far as the diver is concerned, once he has left the board the movements required are identical to those of the Back Dive Straight (Fig. 64). As the body rotates past the peak of the dive, the eyes look for the front end of the board prior to spotting the entry point.

Fig. 67. Reverse Dive Straight

REVERSE DIVE TUCK (*Fig. 68*)

The Take-off   The take-off is similar to that of the Reverse Dive Pike. To allow for the faster rotation when in the tuck position, the angular momentum at take-off is reduced by moving the shoulders back more slowly during the final leg push.

The Flight   As far as the diver is concerned, once he has left the board, the movements required are identical to those of the Back Dive Tuck (Fig. 65).

Fig. 68. Reverse Dive Tuck

INWARD DIVE PIKE (*Fig. 69*)

The Take-off   As the board recoils upwards and the feet give their final push, the hips are moved back, but the shoulders remain over the feet. The feeling is of pulling the abdomen inwards and upwards, the head is kept erect and the hands, arms bent at the elbows, push upwards above the head. The line of thrust from the feet through the hip joint being at an angle to the vertical will result in the body being projected upwards and slightly backwards. As this line of thrust passes to the rear of the body's centre of gravity a turning force will be applied to the body causing inward rotation to appear when the feet leave the board.

The Flight As far as the diver is concerned, once he has left the board, the movements required are identical to those of the Forward Dive Pike (Fig. 60). The fact that in the Inward Dive Pike his centre of gravity is moving backwards, whereas in the Forward Dive Pike it is moving forwards, has no effect on the rotation about the centre of gravity, for

Fig. 69. Inward Dive Pike

the horizontal component of the flight can be ignored. The description of the flight for the Forward Dive Pike therefore may be read in conjunction with the diagram for the Inward Dive Pike.

INWARD DIVE STRAIGHT (*Fig. 70*)

The Take-off   The take-off is similar to that of the Inward Dive Pike (Fig. 69). To obtain the additional angular momentum for the body to rotate in the slower straight position the hips are 'jerked' back faster, through a shorter distance. The piking at take-off is a necessary requirement but should be kept to a minimum.

Plate 24. Agneta Henriksson *(Sweden): Inward Dive Straight*

The Flight   As the feet leave the board, the body is immediately straightened at the hips. As far as the diver is concerned, once he has left the board, the movements required are identical with those of the Forward Dive Straight (Fig. 61) except that he spots the front end of the board before spotting the water.

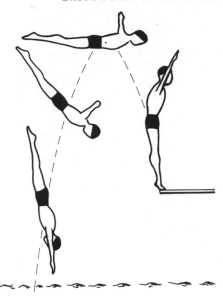

Fig. 70. Inward Dive Straight

Fig. 71. Inward Dive Tuck

INWARD DIVE TUCK (*Fig. 71*)

The Take-off   The take-off is similar to that of the Inward Dive Pike. To allow for the faster rotation when in the tuck position, the angular momentum is reduced by reaching well up with the arms, and by not moving the hips back as far.

The Flight   As far as the diver is concerned, once he has left the board, the movements required are identical to those of the Forward Dive Tuck (Fig. 62) except that he spots the front end of the board before spotting the water.

FORWARD DIVE ½ TWIST STRAIGHT (*Fig. 72*)

The Take-off   The take-off is the same as for a Forward Dive Straight (Fig. 61) except that the shoulders are twisted *slightly* during the final leg push.

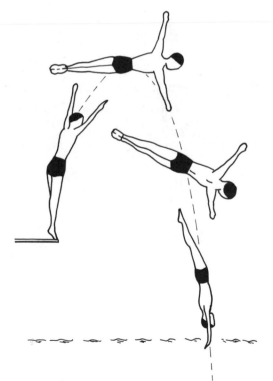

Fig. 72. Forward Dive
½ Twist Straight

Plate 25. Laura Kiveza *(Finland) : Forward Dive ½ Twist Straight*

The Flight   As the feet leave the board the body is straightened at the hips. The arms from the overhead position are taken directly out to the sides at right angles to the body and the eyes look straight ahead. The body rotates (twists) slowly about its long axis so that at the peak of the dive the body is horizontal and on its side, one arm pointing to the water the other pointing upwards. The head is pressed back as the body arches and the body continues to twist on to the back, and the entry is made as in the Back Dive Straight (Fig. 64).

This is a difficult dive to perform well, as both somersault and twist are initiated at take-off. Once in the air, there is little the diver can do to alter the dive. It is a required dive in international competition and has been called the 'great separator' as it is often a decisive factor in determining the final result.

FORWARD DIVE ½ TWIST PIKE (*Fig. 73*)

The Take-off   The take-off is the same as for a Forward Dive Pike (Fig. 60).

Fig. 73. Forward Dive ½ Twist Pike

The Flight The body movements from the moment the feet leave the board, until the pike position is assumed at the peak of the flight, are the same as for a Forward Dive Pike. As the body is unpiked, the shoulders are twisted first, followed by the hips and legs (cat twist) until a half twist has been completed. The feeling is one of turning a large steering wheel with the hands. Throughout the twist the eyes spot the water. The head is pressed back towards the completion of the twist to maintain sight of the water, and the entry is made as in the Back Dive Straight (Fig. 64).

FURTHER PRACTICE

The Inward Dive in the open pike position (Fig. 74) should be practised as an introduction to the more difficult Inward Dive Straight.

Fig. 74. Inward Open Pike Dive

The Back and Reverse Pike take-offs should be practised from the bathside, entering in the inverted pike position (Figs. 75 and 76).

The Back Tuck Jump (Fig. 77) is a useful preliminary to the Back Dive Tuck.

The Reverse Tuck Jump (Fig. 78) is a very useful introduction to the Reverse Dive Tuck.

Fig. 75. Back Pike Drop

Fig. 76. Reverse Pike Drop

Fig. 77. Back Tuck Jump

Fig. 78. Reverse Tuck Jump

Plate 26. Reverse Pike Drop

13. *Laws of Mechanics*

Progress in diving is dependent on an understanding of many principles, but it is important to realize that a knowledge of mechanics is fundamental. As all sport involves movement, an understanding in simple form of the laws governing movement cannot fail to be rewarding.

Mechanics is one of the oldest branches of natural science. The so-called 'laws of mechanics' are the result of careful observation and study of everyday happenings, especially of the way in which things move. We are so familiar with many of these laws that we tend to take them for granted. Mechanics deal with the motion of bodies. The human body in motion whether on land, in the air or in the water has to obey natural laws, whether or not we are aware of the existence of such laws.

In the past much of our technique has been learnt the hard way by a method of trial and error over a prolonged period of time. In many sports it has often been a case of the pupil trying unsuccessfully to perform a movement as the teacher wants it done and, finally, in desperation, succeeding by doing it in the way his intuition suggests.

Diving can be regarded as an art and skilful performers are artists in the true sense of the word. Like all artists their skill is for the most part the result of inherent ability combined with practical experience. A great deal of their art remains a closed book, however, and often their intuition fails to solve the problems involved in the learning of a new skill. It has been the practice of many divers and coaches in the past to rely mainly upon practical experience and it is true to say that in so doing they have inevitably, though unwittingly, conformed with the Laws of Motion. However, due to this lack of knowledge, progress was often slow and painful to the diver.

The fact that the motion of all inanimate objects complies with these well-defined mechanical principles is part of our normal teaching, but few appreciate that the movement of living creatures also complies with the same laws. Were this not so, diving would be extremely simple. If he were able to control his rate of descent, the diver need never experience a painful smack, and he would never have a dive cast over or fall short since he could regulate precisely his speed of rotation. Everyone appreciates that the inevitability of the drop in a dive is a manifestation of natural law; yet it is not widely realized that all other movements follow definite laws which may as readily be explained and applied so that advantage can be taken of what is possible rather than attempting impossibilities.

Many divers and coaches know intuitively the mechanically correct movements necessary to achieve a good dive, but due to the speed of diving movements and the often obscure operation of natural laws even good diving coaches will misinterpret from time to time effects observed and make erroneous assumptions. This will generally retard the rate of progress as effective action cannot be applied to the problems as they arise without a clear understanding of the Laws of Motion.

Laws of Motion   These laws, first expounded by Sir Isaac Newton in 1687, are framed within three main headings.

First Law *(Principle of Inertia)*   A body at rest resists being set in motion, and when set in motion by outside forces, equally resists attempts to alter or stop its motion. The resistance or reluctance to change in the existing state of a body moving in a *straight line* (linear movement) is termed *Inertia*. When the body is *rotating* about an axis this resistance to change is termed the *Moment of Inertia*.

Second Law *(Principle of Acceleration)*   A force acting on a body produces either an acceleration (constant increase of velocity) or a deceleration (constant decrease of velocity). The force of gravity produces an acceleration (or deceleration) of 32 feet (9.80 m) per second for every second it acts on a body. The change in velocity of the body is proportional to the magnitude of the force acting on it.

Third Law *(Principle of Equal and Opposite Reactions)*   Every action produces an opposite reaction of equal momentum. An outstretched arm can only be moved across the body by virtue of the fact that the muscle responsible for moving the arm is attached to the trunk, which will *react* by moving towards the arm with equal *momentum*. When the feet are fixed to the earth (or diving board) the trunk and the earth rotate in theory towards the arm. The mass of the earth is so great however that its velocity is so small as to be for all practical purposes non-existent.

Definitions   The following definitions are given for reference. They are further expounded with practical examples in the succeeding chapters.

Mass: The quantity of matter in a body.
Weight: A measure of the effect of the force of gravity on the mass of an object.
Gravity: The force exerted by the pull of the earth on all matter.
Centre of Gravity: The point through which the force of gravity seems to act (the balance point).

Motion: Movement either in a straight line (translation or linear) or in a circle (rotation or angular).

Momentum: A measure of the 'amount' of translatory motion possessed by a body. It is a product of the mass of the body and its velocity when moving along a straight or curved path.

Velocity: Speed in a given direction.

Angular Momentum: A measure of the amount of 'rotary momentum' possessed by a body by virtue of its rotation about a particular axis. It is a product of the *moment of inertia* of the body and its *angular velocity* about the axis.

Moment of Inertia: A measure of the amount of rotational inertia or resistance about an axis, presented by a body to alteration in its angular velocity. It is the sum of the products of each particle of mass of the body and the 'square of its distance' (radius^2) from the axis of rotation (Fig. 79).

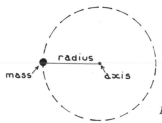

Fig. 79. Moment of Inertia = Mass × Radius^2

Angular Velocity: The rate of rotation of a body about an axis. It varies with alteration to the moment of inertia. It can be measured in degrees or revolutions and is a measure of the angular distance travelled in a unit of time.

Conservation of Angular Momentum: During the flight, the angular momentum stored in the body remains constant about the axis of rotation, *irrespective of any change the diver may make to his body position*. The angular momentum stored in a rotating body is a product of its moment of inertia about the axis of rotation and its angular velocity about that axis. If the moment of inertia (the resistance to rotation) is increased in any way, then the angular velocity will decrease in direct proportion, and likewise if the moment of inertia is decreased, then the angular velocity will automatically increase in proportion in order that the angular momentum remain constant in accordance with the First Law of Motion.

14. *Body Movement in Free Fall*

All movement follows well-defined laws of motion, and whilst many people apply these laws to inanimate objects they refuse to believe that human beings need to obey them. The human body is a wonderful piece of mechanism. That which is responsible for keeping it working is still not fully understood, but when it is moving it becomes basically a series of levers operated by power units in the form of muscles, and any movement made is in accordance with the accepted laws of motion.

Muscle Action   Movement of a limb (lever) about a joint is achieved by the co-ordinated action of various muscle groups. The muscles are attached to the limbs across the joint, and by contraction can move the limbs about the joint. Muscles work in pairs on either side of the limbs, flexing (bending) and extending (straightening) the joint. On contraction, the muscle shortens, bringing the two ends closer together, and likewise the limbs or part of the body to which the muscle is attached. This conforms to the Third Law of Motion, i.e. to every action there is an opposite reaction of equal momentum. It is not possible to move a limb without movement of the part to which the other end of the muscle is attached.

Basic Principles

I. A body in free fall is *always* balanced about its centre of gravity. It may not be *symmetrical*, i.e. one arm may be up and the other extended sideways, but whether moving or still the body is always in a state of stable equilibrium; it can never be off-balance.

II. It requires two opposing forces to create an unbalanced state, and while free in the air there is only one force operative, that is the force of gravity, acting equally on every part of the body.

III. During free fall, the total movement of the trunk or limbs is made in relation to the centre of gravity in accordance with the Third Law of Motion. When the arm is extended sideways some other part of the body will react by moving in the opposite direction keeping the body balanced about the centre of gravity.

IV. The centre of gravity follows a fixed trajectory and it is not possible to alter the flight path of the centre of gravity by any action made by the diver.

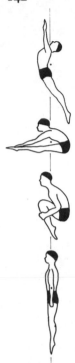

Effects of Change in Position The centre of gravity is an imaginary point about which the body is said to be balanced; it is not necessarily within the body itself. In a close pike position it is approximately 5 inches (130 mm) in front of the hips and in the hollow-back position approximately 1 inch (25 mm) behind the body. When a diver drops from the 10 metre board and assumes the hollow-back, pike, tuck, and straight positions one after the other, he will enter the water feet first with his body vertical. Figure 80 shows the position of the body in relation to the vertical at each stage. In the pike position the legs would be horizontal and the trunk inclined forward at an angle of approximately 30° from the vertical. The hips move back as the body assumes the pike position – the centre of gravity remaining on the line of flight.

It is not within the diver's power to keep his legs vertical and bend his trunk downwards, or to keep his trunk vertical and raise his legs. The only action within the diver's control is to contract his hip flexor muscles, and move his legs and trunk towards one another, the pivot being the hip joint. The relative distances covered by each is dependent on their respective moments of inertia (resistance to rotation) and not on the wishes of the diver.

*Fig. 80. The centre
of gravity remains
on the line of flight*

Assessing the Moment of Inertia When changing from the straight to the pike position, the trunk and legs rotating at the hip joint move towards each other with equal angular momentum. The angular distance travelled will therefore depend on the moment of inertia (mass × radius²) of each part about the hip joint. The greater the moment of inertia (resistance) the slower the part will move and less distance it will travel in a given time.

To assess *accurately* the moment of inertia of the upper trunk and legs about the hip joint is very difficult as each particle of mass must be multiplied by the square of its distance from the hip joint, and added together. The smaller the particles chosen the more accurate the result.

As we are dealing with an imaginary average diver, we are concerned only with relative differences and extreme accuracy is not required.

Changing from Straight to Pike   By dividing an articulated figure of a 10 stone diver into 1 stone units we can add the 'square of the distance of each unit' of the upper body from the hip joint to arrive at an approximate moment of inertia, for the trunk about the hips. We do the same with the legs, and find that the moment of inertia of the upper body about the hip joint is about three times that of the legs. Therefore, when changing from the straight to the pike position, the legs will move three times as fast and cover three times the angular distance (90°) to that of the trunk (30°) leaving an angle of about 60° between. This is the position we *expect* to see in a good pike jump (Fig. 81).

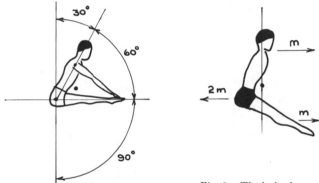

Fig. 81. The Pike Jump position

Fig. 82. The body shape alters, but the centre of gravity remains still

Redistribution about the Centre of Gravity   When changing from the straight to pike position, the centre of gravity remains fixed in space. The shoulders and legs move forward of the centre of gravity and the hips move back, maintaining the balance of the body about the centre of gravity (Fig. 82).

The combined forward linear momentum of the head and shoulders (m) and that of the feet (m) is equal to the rearward linear momentum of the hips (2m). The resultant movement of the centre of gravity being zero. When the straight position is resumed the above actions are reversed.

Muscle Work in the Pike Jump   Because of similar experiences on land, it is sometimes thought that great strength is required in the hip flexor muscles to hold the legs in the pike position shown in Fig. 81. When holding this position on parallel bars there are two opposing forces: the parallel bars acting in effect upwards (reaction R) and the force of gravity acting downwards. The trunk hangs on the arms but the legs are extended forwards and held in position by the hip flexors. Gravity is acting on each part of the body. The arms prevent the trunk from falling and the hip flexors resist the weight (W) of the legs. It requires considerable strength in the hip flexors to maintain this position (Fig. 83).

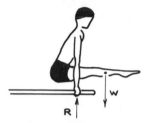

Fig. 83. The Pike position on parallel bars is difficult to hold

When this pike position is assumed in the air little strength is required to raise the legs and none at all to maintain the pike position. This is because there is only one force, the force of gravity, acting on the body whilst it is in free fall. It will be found that girls and women are able to perform pike jumps quite easily, but find the same position on the parallel bars difficult to hold.

Muscle Work in the Inverted Pike   When the body assumes the pike sit-up position on the gym floor it cannot be maintained for long

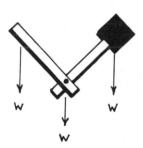

Fig. 84. The Pike Sit-up position is difficult to hold

Fig. 85. Proof that the Pike position in the air is easy to hold

because of the considerable strain on the hip flexors and abdominals (Fig. 84). The pull of gravity on the legs and trunk is resisted by the hip flexor muscle. The reaction of the gym floor, in effect acting upwards, keeps the hips in position against the pull of gravity.

When performing a Back or Reverse Dive in the pike position it is often believed that the extra weight of the head, shoulders and trunk will cause the body to drop backwards if the hip flexor muscles are relaxed, so leaving the legs in the air in the same position as at the peak of the dive. This can be easily disproved in practice by having two sticks loosely pivoted together at one end. A heavy weight is attached to the free end of one of the sticks, and when they are then held in a position similar to the Back Pike Dive and allowed to fall to the ground, it will be found that no alteration in the relative position of the two sticks takes place. They reach the ground in precisely the same position as when they were released (Fig. 85).

When the inverted pike position is assumed in the air it requires no muscular action at all to hold it as there is no upward reaction to oppose. This can easily be proved by assuming the position underwater where the body is weightless, the force of gravity being neutralized by the upthrust of the displaced water.

Changing from Straight to Arched Position   When changing from a straight to an arched back position the centre of gravity remains fixed in space. The shoulders and legs move to the rear of the centre of gravity and the hips move forward, maintaining the balance of the body about the centre of gravity (Fig. 86).

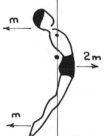

Fig. 86. The body shape alters, but the centre of gravity remains still

The linear momentum of the head and shoulders plus that of the feet must equal the linear momentum of the hips as in the previous example (Fig. 82), therefore the resultant movement of the body as a whole is zero.

With the average diver, the upper trunk will move back through an angle of about 10° and the legs 20°, the pivot being in the lumbar spine. Divers with a flexible spine may be able to increase the movement to about 30° for the upper body and 60° for the legs, i.e. a 90° back bend (see Fig. 134, page 195).

Changing from Straight to Tuck Position   When changing from the straight to the tuck position we find that the angle between the upper legs and the trunk in the tuck position is about 30°. As the body moves into the tuck, the legs bend at the knees so gradually reducing their moment of inertia. A rough approximation would allow for the trunk to move through 20° and the thighs 130°.

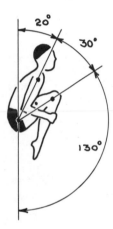

Fig. 87. The Tuck Jump position

This is the position we *expect* to see in a Tuck Jump (Fig. 87). What is not possible, is for the diver to decide to keep his trunk still and raise his legs or vice versa. This is entirely beyond his control. As with the change from straight to pike, the shoulders and legs move forward of the centre of gravity and the hips move back, maintaining the balance of the body about its centre of gravity.

Effect of Horizontal Armswing   When an arm from a sideways extended position is swung across in front of the body, the body will react by moving towards the arm (Fig. 88). The pectoral muscles responsible for the movement pull equally on trunk and arm, but as the moment of inertia (resistance) of the arm about the shoulder joint may be only about a third of that of the rest of the body, the arm will move through an angular distance of about 90° and the trunk and legs only 30°. This can be demonstrated quite easily when standing on a turntable, and

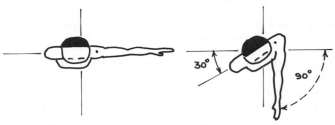

Fig. 88. The trunk reacts by moving towards the arm

also during a jump from a 5 metre board. If the arm is returned to its original position along the same path, the trunk will also return to its starting position. This arm action can be used in certain Twist Dives to turn the trunk. Examples are Back Dive and Reverse Dives with Half Twist (see also Chapter 18).

Effect of Vertical Armswing   When the arms are raised from the sides to a position extended above the head, the body's centre of gravity will rise about 4 inches (100 mm). This can be checked by lying on a see-saw arrangement, first with the arms by the sides, and then with the arms above the head. Fix a belt around the body over the fulcrum position at each test and measure the distance between the belts. When the body is vertical in free fall the centre of gravity cannot be moved in this way. As the arms are raised upwards, the trunk will move downwards 4 inches (100 mm) (Fig. 89). This is of importance in the springboard take-off.

The faster the arms are moved, the greater the upward momentum stored in them. A like amount of *downward* momentum is imparted to the trunk. Whilst this is of little significance during free fall its effect when standing on the end of a springboard is of the utmost importance in depressing the board (see Fig. 103, page 170).

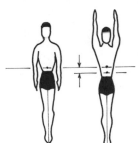

Fig. 89. When the arms are raised, the body lowers, but the centre of gravity remains still

Effect of Arm Circling   A diver who feels himself over-rotating on a feet-first entry will often be seen to circle his arms downwards in front of his body. This action will result in the feet moving forward, i.e. backward rotation of the trunk about the centre of gravity (Fig. 90). For each half circle of the arms, i.e. from above the head to the thighs, the legs will rotate through an angle of about 10°. The muscle responsible for the movement originates in the trunk with the insertion in the upper arm. The arms may be taken up sideways and the action repeated. A diver with very supple shoulders may be able to raise his arms up behind his shoulders and so achieve a continuous circular action. An interesting

Fig. 90. Arm circling
to prevent going over on entry

Fig. 91. Arm circling
to maintain balance

variation of this is observed when a diver is balanced on the front end of the board and starts to topple over. He will *instinctively* start to circle his arms downward in front of his body to stop himself overbalancing (Fig. 91).

The feet cannot move forward due to the friction of the board, so the shoulders move back, the trunk pivoting about the feet.

Effect of Asymmetrical Armswing   When the arms from a sideways extended position are rotated at the shoulder joint, so that one is lowered to the side and one is raised upward, the body will react by moving towards the lowered arm (Fig. 92).

For an 85° movement of the arms, the body will rotate sideways about the centre of gravity through approximately 5°. This effect can easily be demonstrated in a jump from the 5 metre platform. When a full armswing is made starting with one arm up and one down the legs will move through twice the angular distance, i.e. 10° (Fig. 93).

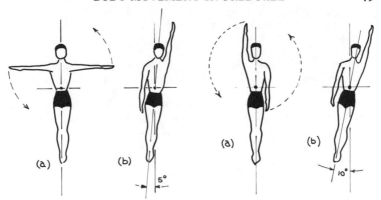

Fig. 92. A half armswing
tilts the body 5°

Fig. 93. A full armswing
tilts the body 10°

These armswing techniques are used to tilt the body about its somer-saulting axis for the initiation of twists (see Chapter 22).

Effect of Pike Twist When the shoulders are turned with the body in the open pike position, the legs will react in the opposite direction (Fig. 94). As the moment of inertia of both legs and hips about an axis through the spine is much greater than that of the upper trunk, arms and head, the legs will move about 10° in one direction, while the trunk moves through 50° in the other. When the body is straightened it will have tilted to one side 10° and the shoulders will be twisted on the spine 50° (Fig. 95). During the straightening the shoulders will also have moved *back* about 20° and the legs moved down about 70°.

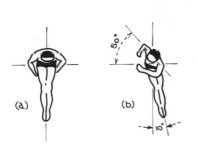

Fig. 94. Twisting the shoulders
against the legs

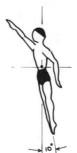

Fig. 95. Tilting the body
by a shoulder twist

This technique is used to great effect to tilt the body about the somer-saulting axis for the initiation of twists. Compare Fig. 93(b) and Fig. 95 (see also Chapter 22, page 227).

Conclusion   To make the result of body movements during the flight of a dive more easily understood, they have been described as if per-formed during either a jump or drop, that is with no rotation. When these body movements are performed while the body is *rotating*, the same principles apply, and the movements of the limbs and trunk pro-duce exactly the same effect. The final result, however, due to the rotation of the body, is more difficult to appreciate and is discussed in the descriptions of the dives concerned. What is not possible is for the diver to start his body rotating continuously in free fall (see Chapter 18).

15. *Time*

Whatever goes up must come down! In no sport is this more appreciated than in diving. It very soon becomes apparent that the more *time* there is available in which to perform the dive, the easier it will be to effect a vertical entry at the end of it.

Taking it up to the 3 metre Board   In the early stages of learning on the 1 metre springboard, there never seems quite enough time to complete the movement, and in an attempt to gain more time the diver is tempted to take the dive up to the 3 metre board. As it is three times the height of the 1 metre board, he feels sure that there must be at least twice as much time available in the air.

At his first attempt from the 3 metre board he decides that he does not want to overdo it, so he takes off rather cautiously – a big mistake. If this painful experience is repeated it soon becomes apparent that there just isn't as much extra time as was at first thought by taking a dive up to a higher board. The question then arises, exactly how much more time is there? Before we can fully appreciate the answer to this question there are a few basic facts that must be understood.

The Effect of Gravity   The greatest force acting against the diver is the force of gravity. Directly he leaves the board and becomes airborne it starts to pull him back again. On his way up it starts to slow him down until eventually for a brief moment he comes to a stop. A state of weightlessness is experienced at this point. This is called the peak of the dive. From this highest point of the flight he falls at a constantly increasing speed (acceleration) caused by the force of gravity, of 32 feet (9.80 m) per second for every second of his drop.

$v = gt$; when 'v' is the velocity in feet or metres per second at any particular moment during the fall, 't' is the time of the fall in seconds at that moment and 'g' is the acceleration due to gravity. After 1 second of fall he will be travelling at 32 ft.p.s. (9.80 m.p.s.) – after 2 seconds, 64 ft.p.s. (19.60 m.p.s.) and so on. This is in accordance with the Second Law of Motion, i.e. force produces acceleration.

Gravity acts equally on all objects, pulling everything towards the earth at the same rate. A man weighing 15 stone (95 kg) and a boy weighing 5 stone (32 kg) both stepping off the 5 metre platform at the same time would both reach the water together.

Consider three 5 stone (32 kg) boys on the 5 metre platform all stepping off at the same time. During the drop two boys clasp hands. This action will obviously make no difference to the rate of fall of either of them. Now consider the same two boys pulling closer together and hugging each other, so that for all intents and purposes they become one mass of 10 stone (63.50 kg). This action again cannot suddenly cause them to travel faster. They will continue to fall at the same rate as the remaining 5 stone (32 kg) boy and so all will reach the water together.

Aristotle (384–322 B.C.) thought that all objects fell to earth at a velocity in proportion to their weight. The belief that heavy objects fell faster than lighter objects was held for many years until Galileo (1564–1643) proved that all objects fell at the same rate. In 1972 an American astronaut demonstrated in the airless conditions on the moon that a feather and a coin fell at the same rate, thus proving for all to see through the media of TV the validity of Galileo's belief.

Effect of Air Resistance   When a cork ball and a steel ball of the same size are dropped from a height of 16 feet (5 m) they both strike the ground at the same time. At distances greater than this the steel ball would in fact, gain slightly on the cork ball. This is due to the resistance of the air, which increases as the square of the speed, i.e. as the speed is doubled the air resistance is increased four times. If the drop was long enough, the increasing air resistance would start to slow down both balls very slightly, but the steel ball, possessing greater momentum, would take longer to slow down so would gain slightly on the lighter ball.

The highest competition diving board is 10 metres, so the maximum drop will be about 35 feet (10.67 m), and the maximum speed achieved at entry will be 33 m.p.h. (53 km.p.h.). From this height and speed, the effect of air resistance on the diver is so slight that it could not be measured and for all practical purposes can be ignored.

Terminal Velocity   If it were possible for a diver to continue his dive in a head-first position, his speed would increase 32 feet (9.80 m) per second for every second of the drop, but eventually the air resistance would become so great that this increase of velocity could not be maintained, until at approximately 150 m.p.h. (240 km.p.h.) the air resistance would balance the increase of speed due to gravity and the body would reach its 'terminal velocity' and would continue to fall at this speed for the rest of the drop.

A sky-diver takes advantage of air resistance by taking up a horizontal position with arms and legs spread. In this position after a drop of about 5.4 seconds he reaches a terminal velocity of about 120 m.p.h. (193 km.p.h.) and is then not conscious of falling as there is no further acceleration. For a diver to reach his terminal velocity of 150 m.p.h.

(240 km.p.h.) he would need to be in the air for 6.8 seconds. This would require a drop of 720 feet (220 m).

The Time Chart   Having discussed the basic principles applying to a free-falling body and some of the practical implications involved, we can from the formula v = gt (when 'v' is the velocity in feet or metres per second, 'g' the acceleration due to gravity of 32 feet (9.80 m) per second, and 't' the time) draw up a chart showing clearly the relationship between the time taken and the distance fallen from the peak of the dive.

1	2	3	4		
	Distance fallen at each $\frac{1}{4}$ second feet (metres)	Total distance fallen feet (metres)	Velocity (v = gt)		
Time in seconds			per second feet (metres)	per hour miles (km)	
0.25	1 (0.30)	1 (0.30)	8 (2.44)	5.50 (9)	
0.50	3 (0.91)	4 (1.22)	16 (4.88)	11 (18)	
0.75	5 (1.52)	9 (2.74)	24 (7.32)	16.50 (26.50)	
1.00	7 (2.13)	16 (4.88)	32 (9.75)	22 (35.50)	
1.25	9 (2.75)	25 (7.62)	40 (12.19)	27.50 (44)	
1.50	11 (3.35)	36 (10.97)	48 (14.63)	33 (53)	
1.75	13 (3.96)	49 (14.93)	56 (17.07)	38.50 (62)	
2.00	15 (4.57)	64 (19.51)	64 (19.51)	44 (71)	

In column one, the time taken falling from the peak of the dive is given at each quarter second.

In column four we have from our formula v = gt the final velocity in feet and metres per second for each period of time (the velocity in m.p.h. and km.p.h. is shown as a matter of interest).

As the acceleration 'g' due to gravity is uniform, the average velocity for any one period of time will be exactly half of the final velocity quoted in column four, i.e. $\frac{1}{2}$ gt.

At any given moment the distance fallen through space, usually denoted as 's', is a product of the average velocity ($\frac{1}{2}$gt) and the time 't' taken, therefore s = $\frac{1}{2}$gt^2 from which we can calculate the distance fallen for each quarter-second period (column three).

Column two gives us an idea of the acceleration. From this we see that the diver falls an extra 2 feet (0.61 m) at each quarter second of his fall. The distance increases as the square of the time (compare columns one and three). When the time of the drop is doubled, the distance fallen increases fourfold. When the time is trebled, the distance fallen increases nine times.

After 0.50 second, the distance fallen is 4 feet (1.22 m). After 1 second, i.e. twice the time, the distance fallen is four times 4 feet, that is 16 feet (4.88 m). After 1.50 seconds the distance fallen is nine times 4 feet, i.e. 36 feet (10.97 m).

Practical Application   From the 3 metre springboard, assuming the diver's centre of gravity rises to a height of 6 feet (1.83 m) above the board, the time taken from the peak of the dive to the water, a drop of 16 feet (4.88 m), would be 1 second. During the first quarter second the body would drop 1 foot (0.30 m) but during the last quarter second it would drop from 9 to 16 feet (2.74 to 4.88 m) so covering 7 feet (2.13 m) in the final quarter second (see Fig. 97).

As the height of the board is increased, the velocity with which the body falls during the latter part of the dive is so great that very little extra time is gained. A drop from the 5 metre board takes 1 second. From 10 metres, the time taken during the drop is nearly 1.50 seconds, so although we have doubled the height, we have only succeeded in gaining half as much time, the last 5 metres being covered in 0.50 seconds (see Fig. 99).

For example, the drop from a height of 20 metres would take about 2 seconds, giving only an extra half second of time for the additional 10 metre drop, the first 10 metres taking 1.50 seconds and the remaining 10 metres being covered in only 0.50 seconds. From this we can see that there would be no advantage in diving from a board higher than 10 metres as the little extra time gained would not be worth having. Taking a dive from a higher board gives a little extra time, but out of all proportion to the height required. This extra height would also increase the velocity at entry, in this instance from 33 m.p.h. (53 km.p.h.) to 44 m.p.h. (71 km.p.h.) and in consequence increase the risk of injury.

We can begin to see that the extra time we are seeking must be obtained by getting more height from the take-off, as extra height gained at the start of the dive 'on the way up' is of greater value than any extra height that can be obtained by adding distance at the end of the dive, which we would get from an increased height of the board.

This can be appreciated more easily by preparing a 'flight chart' from which the advantage of obtaining height *above* the board from the take-off can readily be seen.

The Flight   The flight commences as the feet leave the board at the completion of the take-off and finishes directly any part of the body touches the water. The path taken by the diver during the flight is best studied by considering the path taken by his centre of gravity. When he leaves the board, whether he likes it or not, the path taken by his centre of gravity is beyond his control. He can rotate or twist his body about this point, but no amount of gymnastics on his part can move it from its predetermined line of flight. This, in turn, is determined by the velocity and the angle of protection of the diver's centre of gravity at the moment of take-off, and can for our purpose be resolved into two entirely independent motions at right angles to one another.

Horizontal Motion The first motion in a horizontal direction away from the board is an essential requirement of diving to ensure the diver's safety (see Chapter 17). When the diver has left the board his velocity in a horizontal direction is constant, i.e. the distance travelled is the same for each period of time throughout the dive, it being unaffected by the force of gravity acting at right angles to it. It is also unaffected by any action the diver may make whilst in the air. Once he loses contact with the board this motion will continue beyond his control until he strikes the water.

What is not so obvious is the fact that no amount of movement in a horizontal direction will increase the total time in the air. Time is dependent on *height* alone; forward distance has no effect on the total time available. If, for example, two divers took off from the 5 metre platform at the same instant, one performing a running jump moving in a horizontal direction at take-off, the other just stepping straight down in a vertical direction, they would both reach the water at the same instant (Fig. 96).

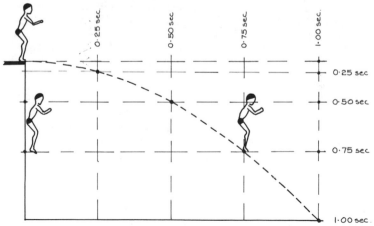

Fig. 96. Both divers will be at the same level, after the same period of time

The diver performing the running jump would land about 30 feet (9.41 m) up the pool, and to cover this extra distance would be travelling faster in a direction along the line of flight from the board to the water. But, irrespective of how far out his forward speed takes him, the time taken from the board to the water is dependent on gravity alone and therefore will be the same irrespective of any forward movement. This is, of course, always supposing that the peak of the dive, i.e. the highest point attained during the flight, is the same in each case. In actual practice, it will be found that the more forward movement there is, the less height attained and therefore less time available (see Chapter 16).

Vertical Motion   The second motion is in a vertical direction, both upwards and downwards. The upward motion obtained from the take-off is one of deceleration due to the pull of gravity acting in the opposite direction. The downward motion is one of acceleration due to this same action of gravity pulling downwards. What is not generally realized is that it takes exactly the same time for the body's centre of gravity to reach the peak of the dive from the take-off as it does to drop from the peak to the same level, and the diver passes this point with exactly the same velocity downwards as the velocity of the take-off was upwards.

The Parabola   The combination of these two motions, both vertical and horizontal, produces a trajectory or line of flight which has a definite form and is called a parabola. The shape of the parabola may vary with different dives but it follows a constant pattern, the form of which is entirely dependent on the angle of projection and the velocity of the diver's centre of gravity at the moment of take-off. The trajectory is symmetrical about a vertical centre line passing through the highest point (peak) of the dive. The shape of the curve on the way up is identical to that on the way down. The time taken to ascend one side of the parabola is also equal to the time taken to descend the other side down to the same level. (Compare Fig. 97 and Fig. 98.)

Springboard Chart, *Good Take-off* (*Fig. 97*)   Using the information given in our time chart, we can reproduce the diver's line of flight quite accurately from the moment that he leaves the board until he reaches the water. To construct this flight chart for a 3 metre springboard we plot both the vertical distance and the horizontal distance travelled in feet against the time taken, in this case after each quarter second of time throughout the dive. Each square on the chart represents 1 foot (0.30 m). Before we can do this we need to know:
    1. The height of the board above the water.
    2. The height of the diver's centre of gravity above the board at the start.

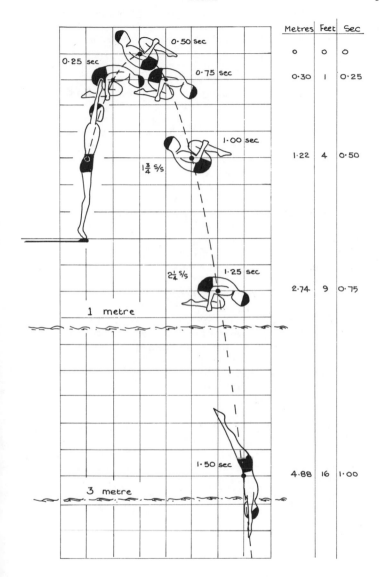

Fig. 97. *Springboard chart – good take-off. Each square represents 1 foot (0·30 m)*

3. The maximum height attained by his centre of gravity during the flight.

4. The horizontal distance from the end of the board to the point of entry.

From this information the total time taken to perform the dive and the horizontal velocity can be calculated. The average diver's centre of gravity is approximately 3 feet (0.91 m) from his feet. From a good springboard take-off his centre of gravity may rise approximately 4 feet (1.22 m) at the peak of his dive. This will take 0.50 seconds, because it takes the same time to *rise* 4 feet to the peak of the dive as it does to *drop* 4 feet (see column three of the time chart on p. 153). From the peak he will drop 16 feet (4.88 m) in 1 second and will be 1 foot (0.30 m) above water-level. This gives a total time in the air of 1.50 seconds, that is 0.50 seconds going up and 1 second coming down. If he enters the water at a point approximately 6 feet (1.83 m) from the front end of the board, his horizontal velocity will be 6 feet (1.83 m) in 1.50 seconds, i.e. 4 feet (1.22 m) per second, or 1 foot (0.30 m) for each quarter second of his flight time.

The first two columns on the right-hand side of the springboard chart (Fig. 97) indicate the distance fallen for each quarter second of the drop. We construct the flight parabola by plotting the position of the diver's centre of gravity at each quarter second period of time during the flight.

Springboard Chart, *Poor Take-off* (*Fig. 98*)   A similar chart can be drawn to represent the line of flight resulting from a rise at take-off of only 1 foot (0.30 m) as performed by an inexperienced diver. We can compare his dive with that of the expert who achieved a 4 foot (1.22 m) rise as shown in the springboard chart, Fig. 97. When we compare the two charts, we see that from the 3 metre springboard, after 1 second of his flight, the expert is 3 feet (0.91 m) *above* the board (13 feet or 3.96 m above the water) with 0.50 seconds to go. But the diver with the poor take-off after 1 second, is 5 feet (1.52 m) *below* the board (5 feet above the water) with only 0.20 seconds to go. After 1.25 seconds of the flight has been passed, the expert is 2 feet (0.61 m) below the board with 8 feet (2.44 m) still to go, but the inexperienced diver after 1.25 seconds is 2 feet (0.61 m) below the surface of the water! The expert obtaining a rise of 4 feet (1.22 m) from the take-off is in the air for approximately 1.50 seconds from the 3 metre board. The diver with a rise of only 1 foot (0.30 m) would have to take off from a 7 metre springboard to obtain the same amount of time in the air, as is clearly shown in the firmboard chart (see Fig. 99).

The Angle of Take-off   In Fig. 97, the expert's angle of take-off is 14° and he rises 4 foot (1.22 m) and enters the water 6 foot (1.83 m) from

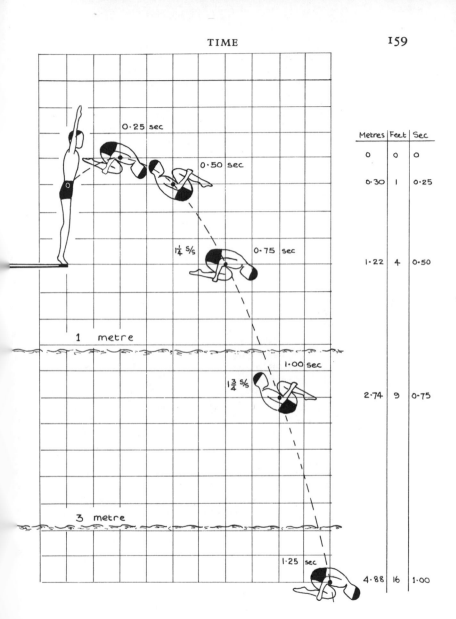

Fig. 98. Springboard chart – poor take-off. Each square represents 1 foot (0.30 m)

the front end of the board, his time in the air being 1.5 seconds. The inexperienced diver leans forward excessively so that his angle of take-off is 45°. He rises only 1 foot (0.30 m) and enters the water nearly 10 feet (3 m) out. His time in the air is only 1.2 seconds (Fig. 98). From a study of Figs. 97 and 98 it becomes apparent that the expert is in the air longer using a 1 metre springboard than the other diver is using the 3 metre springboard. The expert has as much time from take-off to board level, as the beginner has for a complete dive from the 3 metre board. (See also Chapter 16 and Figs. 100 and 101, page 166.)

Flight Comparisons   When comparing conditions between a 3 metre and a 1 metre dive, the desired number of rotations would be related logically to the respective flight times, not distances. A diver using a good springboard can raise his centre of gravity about 4 feet (1.22 m) from the take-off. The important fact is that it will take exactly the same amount of time to rise up 4 feet, i.e. 0.50 second, as it will to drop 4 feet from the peak of the dive. This means that, from the 1 metre spring-board, when his centre of gravity has dropped from the peak of the dive to a position level with his take-off point, which will be about 3 feet (1 m) above board level, 1 second out of a total time of 1.25 seconds will have passed. This leaves only 0.25 second to drop the remaining 6 feet (1.83 m) to the water. This makes it obvious that the greater part of the dive must be performed above board level.

The increase in height that can be gained during the take-off is more readily obtained from the springboard than from the firmboard. So we find that the time in the air obtained from the 1 metre springboard is nearly the same as that from the 5 metre platform. An increase of 2 feet (0.61 m) in the height of the take-off from the 1 metre springboard will give an extra 0.23 second of time. To gain the same increase of time by taking the dive from a higher board would require an extra 6 feet (1.83 m), of height, i.e. from the 3 metre springboard. A diver with a good take-off from the 3 metre springboard is in the air for 1.50 seconds. The same diver on the 1 metre springboard performing the same dive is in the air for 1.25 seconds. There is just 0.25 second, i.e. one-fifth of the total time longer on the 3 metre springboard than on the 1 metre – just time enough to provide a more comfortable drop or a better finish to the dive.

The 2½ Somersault from the 3 Metre Board (*see Fig. 97*)   To obtain a stretched entry from a 2½ Somersault from the 3 metre spring-board, a good diver must allow at least 0.25 second from his total time of 1.50 seconds for 'coming out'. This means that he must be in a head-down tucked position ready to come out after 1.25 seconds, i.e. 2 feet (0.61 m) below board level (8 feet or 2.44 m above water-level). This gives him 1.25 seconds in which to perform the $2\frac{1}{2}$ Somersault, a rotation of half a somersault in each of the remaining quarter-second periods.

For a diver practising on the 1 metre springboard, it would be necessary for him to perform a $1\frac{1}{2}$ Somersault and be in the *head-down* position ready to come out after 0.75 second (6 feet or 1.83 m above board level, 9 feet or 2.74 m from the water), to get the correct feeling of the take-off for the $2\frac{1}{2}$ Somersault from 3 metres. If he preferred to practise the Double Somersault on the 1 metre, he must be round facing front, ready to step out into the water after 1 second (3 feet or 0.91 m above board level). Again, if he wishes to hang on to the tuck, he must be in the *head-down* tuck position on entering the water, having performed $2\frac{1}{2}$ revolutions after a time of 1.25 seconds. It is advisable to keep the eyelids tightly closed if choosing this method on the 1 metre board.

From the foregoing, it becomes apparent that most 3 metre dives can be performed on the 1 metre springboard. It is also obvious that a diver must be able at least to get 'his head in' from the 1 metre, before taking the dive up to the 3 metre. When he takes the dive from the 3 metre he will then have only 0.25 second longer in which to straighten his body for the entry.

Firmboard Chart (*Fig. 99*)   By the same procedure it is possible to construct a firmboard chart. The chart shows the line of flight with each quarter second period of time marked at the appropriate position along the curve. The water-levels are shown for the 1, 3, 5, $7\frac{1}{2}$ and 10 metre boards. The height assumed in the take-off is 1 foot (0.30 m), which is a fair average figure from a firmboard. On some running dives a good performer may obtain a rise of as much as 2 feet (0.63 m). On the other hand, anyone who has stood on the same platform as a diver will know that many divers do not rise at all – they just disappear over the edge.

There is usually more 'lean' on take-off from a running dive from a firmboard than from a springboard, so we find that the horizontal movement away from the board is greater. In the firmboard chart it is 2 feet (0.61 m) per quarter second as compared with 1 foot (0.30 m) in the springboard flight chart (Fig. 97).

The poor take-off from the springboard (Fig. 98) results in a line of flight identical to that of Fig. 99.

The $3\frac{1}{2}$ Somersault from 'Ten' (*see Fig. 99*)   When calculating the possibility of performing the $3\frac{1}{2}$ Somersault from the 10 metre platform, ideally we should allow at least the last 0.25 second for 'coming out'. This would mean being in a face-down 'kneeling' position, having completed $3\frac{1}{4}$ somersaults ready to come out, 12 feet (3.66 m) above the water-level after 1.50 seconds. Allowing for the fact that the upper trunk will perform a quarter somersault during the take-off phase, before the feet leave the board, this leaves us with three somersaults to complete in 1.50 seconds, i.e. one somersault each half second.

Working back, we would be in the $2\frac{1}{4}$ Somersault position after 1 second, 5 feet (1.52 m) below the board. This point is also nearly 12 feet (3.66 m) above the 5 metre water-line, so we must be able to perform a $2\frac{1}{2}$ Somersault from 5 metres in order to perform a $3\frac{1}{2}$ Somersault from the 10 metre platform. Moving backwards up the flight chart still further, we should be in the $1\frac{1}{4}$ Somersault position at 0.50 second, 3 feet (0.91 m) above the board. This means that in order to get the right take-off and feeling of the spin required for a $3\frac{1}{2}$ Somersault from the 10 metre platform, the diver should be able to perform a running $1\frac{1}{2}$ Somersault from the bathside.

If he can do this, then, providing he has the necessary nerve of course, he has the correct take-off and therefore will be able to perform successfully a $3\frac{1}{2}$ Somersault from the 10 metre platform and, of course, a $2\frac{1}{2}$ Somersault from the 5 metre board.

The Inward $2\frac{1}{2}$ from 'Ten' (*see Fig. 99*) We will assume we aim to be in a head-down tuck position ready to stretch for the entry after 1.50 seconds, as before. In order to perform the Inward $2\frac{1}{2}$ Somersault we need to perform approximately half a somersault during each quarter second period working back from this point. Therefore at the 1 second position we must be head down having performed a $1\frac{1}{4}$ Somersault.

We can also see from the chart that if we can perform an Inward $1\frac{1}{2}$ Somersault coming out at this point from the 3 metre firmboard then we have the right take-off for the Inward $2\frac{1}{2}$ Somersault from 10 metres.

Working back farther, we must be round in the Inward $\frac{3}{4}$ Somersault position at a board level after 0.75 second of the flight. This leaves 0.50 second for the first $\frac{1}{2}$ Somersault because we must allow for less height and a slower rate of spin whilst going into the tuck position from an inward take-off.

Dive Analysis It is often helpful when analysing a dive to locate the half-way point on the flight curve. It is important to remember that it is half-way in *time* and not *distance* that is required. In the case of the $3\frac{1}{2}$ Somersault from the 10 metre board, assuming that you are ready to stretch for the entry after 1.50 seconds, then at least half of the dive must be completed at the 0.75 second position at board level, this being the true half-way point on the flight curve. This means that at least $1\frac{1}{2}$ somersaults must have been performed at this point, showing the necessity of being able to perform a $1\frac{1}{2}$ Somersault from the bathside in order to get the correct 'feel' of the take-off.

By laying a sheet of tracing paper over the charts, the diver's body positions at the various time-allocation points along the line of flight can

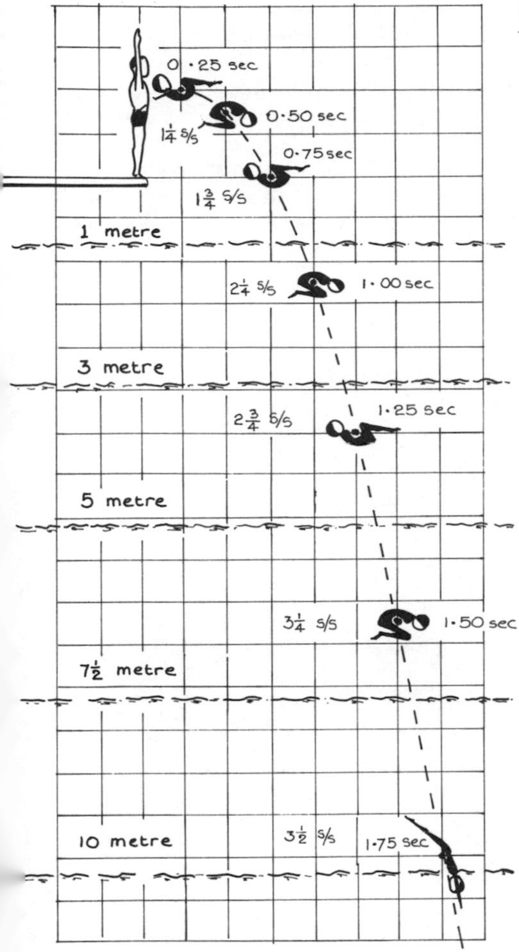

Metres	Feet	Sec	(Inward 2½)
o	o	o	
0·30	1	0·25	¼
1·22	4	0·50	¾
2·74	9	0·75	1¼
4·88	16	1·00	1¾
7·62	25	1·25	2¼
10·97	36	1·50	2½

Fig. 99. Firmboard chart. Each square represents 2 feet (0·61 m)

be drawn in, and it soon becomes apparent exactly how far round he needs to be at each point in order to complete the dive.

Conclusion   In order to achieve the time in which to complete a dive satisfactorily we need to project the body upwards. Height above the board will give the correct trajectory.

A diver's early training should allow him to concentrate on and consolidate this essential feature. If he is rushed too soon into difficult dives he may unwittingly be forced to sacrifice height in a natural desire to 'get into the dive' early.

16. *Obtaining Height*

The time available during the flight is one of the most important factors in the successful performance of the more difficult multiple somersaulting and twisting dives. This essential time can only be obtained by projecting the body *upwards* at take-off. Apart from any other requirement at take-off, the successful completion of the dive depends on the height the body rises above the board, as height alone is related to time. To achieve this objective, the diver must have a clear understanding of the mechanics of the take-off, and the ability to apply it successfully, in order to obtain the height required.

Due to the varying positions of the body at the peak of the dive, height is always measured from the body's centre of gravity and is given as height above board level. In this way direct comparison may be made between various boards irrespective of their height above the water.

Basic Principles

I. The more height a diver can obtain from his take-off the longer time he will have in which to perform his dive.

II. For a given angle of take-off, the height obtained is dependent upon the upward velocity of the diver at the moment of leaving the board which itself depends entirely on the use the diver makes of his available energy.

Effective Velocity   In Fig. 97 the downward velocity of the expert at 3 feet (0.91 m) above board level is 16 feet (4.88 m) per second (see the time chart on p. 153). This also represents his upward velocity (v), at take-off (Fig. 100). The horizontal velocity (H) is 4 feet (1.22 m) per second. The resultant projected velocity (P) is 16.70 feet (5.09 m) per second, the angle of take-off being 14°.

In Fig. 98 the downward velocity of the weak diver at 3 feet (0.91 m) above board level, is only 8 feet (2.44 m) per second. This also represents his upward velocity at take-off (Fig. 101). In this case the horizontal velocity (H) is 8 feet (2.44 m) per second. The resultant projected velocity (P) is 11.20 feet (3.41 m) per second, and the angle of take-off 45°.

Although the *projected* velocity of the weak diver is 11.20 feet (3.41 m) per second, his low angle of take-off results in an *effective* vertical velocity of only 8 feet (2.44 m) per second, producing a rise of only 1 foot, (0.30 m). The expert with less lean at take-off, i.e. only 14° from vertical, has

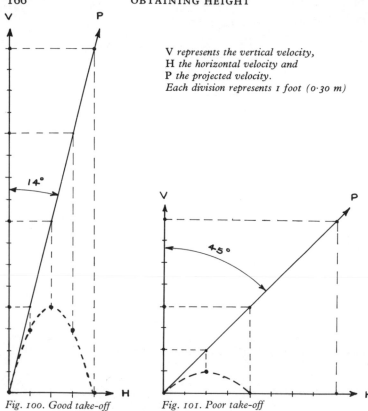

V *represents the vertical velocity,*
H *the horizontal velocity and*
P *the projected velocity.*
Each division represents 1 foot (0·30 m)

Fig. 100. Good take-off   Fig. 101. Poor take-off

an effective vertical velocity of 16 feet (4.88 m) per second, only 0.70 foot (0.21 m) per second less than his projected velocity, producing a rise of 4 feet (1.22 m). From this analysis we see the importance of an upright take-off in obtaining height above the board.

The Standing Firmboard Take-off   From a firmboard, the diver's energy is used first in overcoming his inertia by extending his body from a slight crouch position against the pull of gravity. He extends his hips, knees and ankles as vigorously as possible in order to accelerate the rise of the body so that he leaves the board with the greatest possible velocity. The *faster* the extension of the legs and feet, the greater the take-off velocity.

If the arms are swung upwards in time with the leg extension, momentum will be stored in them. At the completion of the armswing, this momentum will be transferred to the rest of the body assisting its rise from the board. In the firmboard take-off every action the diver makes and the whole of his energy is directed into springing away from the board.

The Running Firmboard Take-off   More height can be obtained from a running two-foot take-off than from a standing take-off. The run is performed at a controlled accelerated rate, each step being faster than the one before. Taking off from one foot, the diver performs a low hop and lands with both feet together, with the body bent at the hips, knees and ankles, which are then extended vigorously, projecting him upwards and outwards.

When he lands from the hop, the kinetic energy from the drop is absorbed in the springing muscles of the hip, knees and ankles, putting them 'on the stretch'. When a muscle is subjected to a sudden strong extension in this way it reacts by contracting rapidly, much faster than is possible by any *conscious* contraction, as in a standing take-off. For this reason it is possible to obtain greater height from a running-take-off than a standing one. In order to obtain height the run must be controlled. Too fast a run will give too much forward momentum to the body at take-off, causing excessive lean with reduced height and unnecessary forward travel.

Maintaining Forward Momentum   The object of the run is to overcome the body's inertia before the actual take-off. Having set the body in motion, the aim then is to project as much as possible of the forward momentum upward into the take-off. In this way, the whole of the body's energy can be utilized in the spring. The diver usually lands on the end of the board with a slight backward lean. As he goes into the crouch his centre of gravity moves over his feet, and at the moment of take off his hips are above his feet with his centre of gravity beyond the

Fig. 102. The centre of gravity moves forward during the spring at take-off

front end of the board (Fig. 102). This ensures that there is no interruption to the forward momentum of the centre of gravity during the final landing and take-off from the end of the board.

The Use of the Springboard A springboard is a device for storing energy and converting it into a useful force to enable a diver to obtain more height than is possible from a firmboard. The more a springboard is deflected the greater will be the potential energy stored in the board and the more powerful will be its recoil. The aim, therefore, is to depress the board as far as possible.

The more flexible the board the easier it is to depress it and store energy, but the longer will be the time taken to deflect it in order to store this energy. With the older stiffer type of board this deflection time was usually much less than the diver's springing time. The faster the diver extends his legs the greater will be the force applied against the board to depress it, but there is a limit to how quickly a diver can extend his legs.

If he is to make full use of his springing power he must be given sufficient *time* in which to do it. If the board is too 'stiff' its deflection time will be too short and the diver will have insufficient time in which to use his energy in depressing the board. He will be unable to store energy in it and will therefore gain very little assistance from it.

Take-off from a Rising Board With the modern flexible board, the time taken for it to reach its lowest point can be much longer than the time it takes a diver to extend his legs and feet in the spring and he would usually call it too soft. If the diver is to spring upwards with the maximum velocity his *final* push must be made against a *rising* board. If the board is still going down when his legs and feet are fully extended his take-off velocity, and therefore his height during the flight, will be reduced. By adjusting the position of the fulcrum a diver is able to select a position which affords him the optimum period of time in which to depress and spring from the board.

When the fulcrum is moved *towards* the front end of the board, the time taken for one complete deflection is *reduced*, i.e. the board moves faster. When the fulcrum is moved *away* from the front end of the board, the swinging time is *increased* and the board moves more slowly. For a given position of the fulcrum, the time remains the same for any deflection of the board, great or small.

Advantage of a Flexible Board It follows, therefore, that with a greater deflection of the board, the recoil will be faster than for a lesser deflection, the board having to travel a greater distance in the same time. The board reaches its maximum velocity upwards at the midway point of its swing, i.e. the resting position of the board with the diver standing on the front end.

A diver takes advantage of a springboard's capacity to store energy then return it. He finds it is easier to obtain height from a flexible board than from a stiffer board.

The Problem of the Standing Springboard Take-off (*see p. 116*)
In the running take-off the diver can take advantage of the kinetic energy available from the drop to assist him in depressing the board. In the standing take-off from a flexible board the problem becomes more difficult. He must first find some means of setting the board in motion and then, working in time with the swing of the board, try to depress it further by applying a downward force as the board is descending. The simplest method of setting a board in motion is by raising and lowering the heels. To be effective this must be co-ordinated with the swing of the board. Raising the arms upwards will also cause a downward reaction and most divers start the board moving by this method (see Fig. 59a).

On very flexible boards some divers start the board moving with their feet, then raise their arms in time with the descent of the board to depress it further. Once the diver has succeeded in setting the board in motion by the preliminary use of his feet and arms, he must then try to depress the board to its maximum on its downward swing. If the board is very flexible he cannot do this with his leg push alone, he must use his arms.

Use of the Arms in Depressing the Board As the board is approaching the top of its swing (see Fig. 59b), from a position above head level the diver will swing his arms down sideways and backwards in a circular movement, at the same time going into a deep crouch position (see Figs. 59c and d). This will relieve the weight on the board. His arms will swing from behind, past his hips, then upwards in front of his body (see Fig. 59e). As his hands pass the hips his body weight will depress the board. The faster he swings his arms upwards, the greater will be the momentum stored in them. The result of this arm action, will be a force of equal and opposite momentum applied downwards against the board as it descends under his weight. By swinging his arms up vigorously a diver can create a reaction downwards equal to that of his own body weight. The maximum reaction to the armswing occurs when the arms are horizontal, at which point the board is nearing maximum deflection (Fig. 103).

On a firmboard this will be resisted, but when performed on a springboard the board will be depressed. The more flexible the board the more important does the armswing become as a means of depressing the board. This can easily be demonstrated while standing on bathroom scales.

Fig. 103. The upward armswing depresses the board

Use of the Legs in Depressing the Board As his arms swing upwards, he will start to extend his legs vigorously against the board, imparting upward momentum to the trunk. This leg drive, if performed correctly, will result in a force of equal and opposite momentum downwards against the already descending board, depressing it still further.

Use of the Legs in Raising the Body As the board recoils, accelerating the body upwards, the legs and feet will complete their extension giving additional acceleration to the body. The board reaches its maximum velocity as it approaches the horizontal, at which point the diver loses effective contact with it.

Advantages of the Running Springboard Take-off (*see p. 110*) In the running take-off from the springboard, the kinetic energy available from the drop from the hurdle will enable the board to be depressed much further than is possible by any preliminary arm and leg movements employed in the standing take-off. For this reason the fulcrum can be placed further back than for a standing take-off, allowing more energy to be stored in the board.

The diver lands on the end of the board *softly*, to avoid any shock with its accompanying loss of kinetic energy, trying not to hinder the descent of his centre of gravity. He does this by flexing his knees and ankles on landing (see Fig. 58f) and then going into a deep crouch position, allowing his weight to depress the board (see Fig. 58g). A common fault is to 'stab' at the board with the feet just prior to landing.

From this position the use of the arms and legs and the mechanics of the take-off are identical to that described for the Standing Springboard Take-off (compare Fig. 58 with Fig. 59).

The Mechanics of the Hurdle The greater the drop from the hurdle, the further the board will be depressed. In the running take-off from the modern flexible springboard, the diver takes advantage of its flexibility to gain extra height in his hurdle step. On his last step into the hurdle, his weight, as it comes over his foot, starts the board moving downwards; the knee is then bent, and the foot, now flat, is pushed against the board. The reaction to this action and to the armswing and opposite knee lift will depress the board further (see Fig. 58c). As the board recoils, projecting him upwards, he extends the knee and ankle vigorously, accelerating his body upwards into the hurdle step (see Fig. 58d).

The mechanics of the hurdle step are identical with those of the take-off from the end of the board except that it is performed from one leg (compare Figs. 58c and 58i). As with the final take-off, extra time is needed to depress a flexible board during the hurdle step. The diver must ensure that he does not swing his arms upwards too soon. As his knee bends, his weight must be over his foot and his arms should be behind his hips ready to swing forwards and upwards (see Fig. 58b).

N.B. When the diver lands from the hurdle step, the board has, by that time, stopped swinging. There is no suggestion of the diver trying to 'catch the swing of the board' as is sometimes believed.

Balance at Take-off The modern springboard is very flexible and can store more energy than the older type of stiff board, but it *takes more time to do it*. The problem confronting the diver is to co-ordinate his movements so that his energy is distributed over a longer period of time, enabling him to depress the board to its maximum, yet to spring away from it as it rises. To obtain the maximum effect from his body weight, armswing and leg drive over the longest period of time, it is essential that the diver's centre of weight (centre of gravity) remains balanced over his feet for as long as possible during the take-off.

In order to deflect the board to its maximum, the diver must remain in balance on the *end* of the board until it is fully depressed, and to obtain the maximum advantage from its recoil he must also remain in balance as it rises. If the body is allowed to lean from the board then only a part of the available forces will be effective. Any body lean at take-off will reduce the effective height obtained from the spring. The greatest height is obtained from a vertical take-off. However, there must be some horizontal motion of the body with every take-off (see Chapter 17). The horizontal motion should be kept to a minimum so that the maximum height can be achieved from the take-off.

17. *Horizontal Motion for Safety*

Travel away from the bathside or board at take-off is one of the most important safety factors to observe when diving. Both teacher and coach must be fully aware of the need for this, and also know how to ensure that this essential action takes place. Diving differs from trampolining in this respect. In diving, horizontal motion away from the point of take-off is essential, but on the trampoline it is neither necessary nor desirable. The aim on a trampoline is to confine any motion to a vertical movement only, so that all stunts can be kept within the area of the bed. When teaching diving to trampolinists, this difference must be stressed to prevent accidents caused through striking the board.

Before his feet leave the board, the diver must set his body moving *away* from the board, to have sufficient space to complete the dive without striking the board as he passes it. In addition to any vertical motion and rotation required, he must impart horizontal motion to his body before his take-off is completed. The linear motion once imparted to the body will cause the body to travel at a constant rate away from the board without any further action on the part of the diver.

Body Alignment at Board Level   The actual distance required to clear the board will depend on the body's alignment in relation to the vertical as the board is passed. With a diver's body in the *vertical* position as he passes the board, his centre of gravity will need to be no more than about 1 foot (0.30 m) in front of the board to provide sufficient clearance. With the body *horizontal* as it passes the board, the centre of gravity will need to be at least 3 feet (1 m) from the board in order to

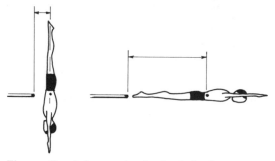

Fig. 104. Board clearance is related to body alignment

clear it sufficiently (Fig. 104). This is one reason why somersaults in the straight position can be more dangerous than somersaults in the more compact tuck position.

Height and Safety A competent diver gaining sufficient height in his dive will have more time at his disposal, and will have completed most of the dive *above* the board so that he is in the near-vertical entry position as he passes the board. A beginner gaining very little height may be only half-way round and be near horizontal at board level, so will need to travel farther out in order to avoid contact with the board. The beginner is often forced to travel away from the board excessively for safety reasons. This excessive travel spoils his take-off, reducing height in the dive and its consequent gain in time. This not only makes the execution of the dive more difficult for the beginner, but also more dangerous.

As confidence increases, more height is obtained in the flight and the dive becomes easier and safe to perform. An example of this is the Reverse Dive. A competent diver achieving reasonable height at take-off will be in a near vertical position on passing the board, but a beginner achieving little height may be near horizontal at board level and stand more chance of striking the board (Fig. 105).

Fig. 105. Height (at take-off) allows greater clearance

Advantage of the Springboard To provide sufficient clearance more lean is usually required with a firmboard take-off than with a take-off from a springboard. The springboard will provide greater *height* in the dive and therefore more *time* to allow the body to rotate nearer to vertical at board level. As the techniques required to initiate travel away from the board depend a great deal on the type of dive being performed, it is necessary to discuss them under the various groups of dives.

Forward Dives Travel away from the board is produced in this group entirely by overbalancing (lean). A natural instinct of self-preservation will usually ensure that the diver leans forward sufficiently as he takes off. With beginners, this lean is usually excessive, causing a variety of faults. As the diver overbalances, his centre of gravity moves beyond his base (feet). Once set in motion his centre of gravity will continue outwards beyond his control (Fig. 106). Lean should be reduced to the minimum consistent with safety requirements.

Angle of Lean   The angle of lean (L) is measured from a line projected from the toes through the body's centre of gravity. When the body is bent forward at take-off, the hips may be over the feet or even slightly behind the feet, but if the centre of gravity is beyond the feet then the body will topple forward (Fig. 107).

Compare Figs. 106 and 107. Although the body positions are different the angle of lean is the same.

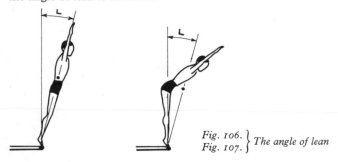

Fig. 106.
Fig. 107. } *The angle of lean*

Back Dives   Travel away from the board in Back Dives is achieved as in Forward Dives, entirely by overbalancing (Fig. 108). Leaning backwards is not a natural movement, so has to be taught to most beginners to avoid the feet striking the board. This is especially so when performing Back Dives from the bathside or firmboard.

During the take-off for Back Dives the body may be arched so that although the hips are above the feet the body's centre of gravity is beyond the edge of the board causing it to topple backwards (Fig. 109).

Fig. 108.
Fig. 109. } *Lean (L) produces travel (T)*

Compare Figs. 108 and 109. Although the body positions are different, the angle of lean is the same, as in the previous example with Forward Dives.

The Effects of Lean   The lean (L) necessary for safety in Forward and Back Dives also produces rotation (R) in the required direction, so assists in the execution of these dives (Figs. 110 and 111). Excessive lean,

Fig. 110. $\Big\}$
Fig. 111. $\Big\}$ *Lean produces positive rotation in Forward and Back Dives*

however, reduces height so should be kept to the minimum necessary for safety and aesthetics.

Any lean (L) at take-off in Reverse or Inward Dives produces rotation (R) in the wrong direction, making the correct execution of these dives more difficult (Figs. 112 and 113). Some lean may be desirable when

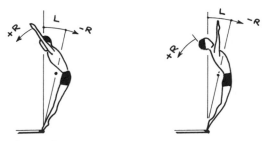

Fig. 112. $\Big\}$
Fig. 113. $\Big\}$ *Lean produces negative rotation in Inward and Reverse Dives*

teaching these dives to beginners, especially from the bathside or firm-board, but should be eliminated as the correct take-off technique is mastered.

Reverse Dives   Travel away from the board in Reverse Dives is produced by momentum (M) imbalance (Fig. 114). As the feet push downward against the board the head and shoulders (M1) are moved backwards and the hips, lower trunk and upper legs (M2) move forward. Were the body in free fall, the feet would move backwards, the centre of gravity remaining still (see Fig. 86).

During the take-off the feet are prevented from moving back by the friction of the board. As the mass of the hips etc. are about twice that of the shoulders and head, a momentum imbalance is produced, resulting in the body moving forwards as the feet leave the board.

Fig. 114. Momentum imbalance produces travel in Reverse Dives

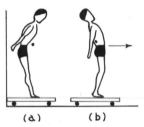

(a)   (b)

Fig. 115. Reverse take-off experiment

Reverse Experiment   This can be proved quite easily with the aid of a wheeled or sliding platform (Fig. 115). The diver stands on the platform, which should be touching the wall behind to prevent backward travel. Ideally the platform should be on wheels or rollers to reduce friction to a minimum. If this is not possible then sheets of paper placed beneath a square of plywood will often suffice. The diver takes up the hips-bent position shown at (a), then jerks his shoulders back, moving his hips forward at the same time, until he is standing upright. He will find that the trolley will travel forward immediately the body movement is completed (b).

To provide further proof of the validity of the experiment the diver should perform the same movements with the trolley *away* from the wall. He will find that no movement of the trolley results. This is a demonstration of the result of the action if performed in free fall (see Chapter 14).

Inward Dives   Backward travel in Inward Dives is achieved by momentum (M) imbalance as in Reverse Dives (Fig. 116). As the feet push downward against the board the head and shoulders (M1) move forward, and the hips, lower trunk and upper legs (M2) move backward.

Were the body in free fall, the feet would move forward, the centre of gravity remaining still (see Fig. 82). During the take-off the feet are prevented from moving forward by the friction of the board as in Reverse Dives.

As in the Reverse take-off, the mass of the hips, etc. being twice that of the head and shoulders results in the body moving backwards as the feet leave the board.

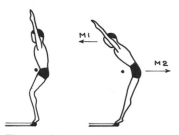

Fig. 116. Momentum imbalance produces travel in Inward Dives

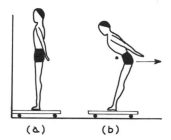

(a)   (b)

Fig. 117. Inward take-off experiment

Inward Experiment   As with the Reverse Dive, inward travel can be verified with the trolley experiment (Fig. 117). The diver stands upright on the trolley, facing the wall, trolley touching the wall as before (a).

He then moves his shoulders forward and his hips back until he is in the hips-bent position. The trolley will travel away from the wall immediately the body movement is completed (b). The experiment should then be repeated with the trolley *away* from the wall and it will be found impossible to set the trolley in motion. This demonstrates the effect of the action if performed during free fall.

Conclusion   Knowledge of the techniques required to produce linear motion away from the board will give added confidence to diver, teacher and coach. This is especially so with the Reverse and Inward groups in which the essential action is not easily apparent to the observer. An understanding of the principles involved will prevent time being wasted and avoid frustration on the part of both diver and teacher.

18. *Creating Rotation*

It is an amazing fact that divers have for years been somersaulting in the air during their dives without knowing how they do it! When asked, a diver will describe how he *thinks* he performs the dive. For a single somersault he usually says that he takes off reaching up, then at the top of the dive drops his head forward to start himself somersaulting. When he has rotated far enough he presses his head and shoulders back to stop the rotation.

The speed of movement at take-off is so great that it is not possible for the human eye to assess accurately what has taken place. It is only since the advent of cine films, used in slow-motion, that it has been possible to analyse the movements that do occur. It is possible to improve one's own performance by watching a film and imitating the actions of a diver who performs a movement well. However, to the untrained eye it is very difficult to observe what is actually happening in a dive, even in slow-motion. It is only a knowledge of what *cannot* happen that enables the observer to make a clear assessment of the performance.

It is sometimes thought that during the flight of the dive the head, being a heavy object at one end of the body, will fall faster than the feet, so causing the body to somersault slowly. This is obviously a fallacy (see Chapter 14). The belief that a diver can start himself rotating by dropping his head, 'causing the body to overbalance', is wishful thinking. This belief was held by coaches for many years. Divers were instructed to wait until the top of the dive was reached before starting the body somersaulting. In actual fact the head plays very little part in the *physical* control of the dive during flight.

Practical Experiments   No action on the part of the diver during a jump can cause him to rotate and enter the water head-first. Whatever he does, when he finally straightens for his entry, he will be in the same position relative to the vertical as when he started the jump (see Fig. 80). A little practical experiment will prove this, though it is possible that it will only silence many of the disbelievers who may go away thinking that they have been tricked.

One has only to ask a diver to perform a series of plain jumps from a 1 metre springboard, telling him to enter head first when he hears you call. Let him perform the first two without a call until you are sure that he is performing a jump, i.e. no rotation. The antics he will get up to when you do call, have to be seen to be believed. But whatever he does, he will find it impossible to create the smallest amount of rotation and will always enter feet first.

Popular Beliefs If dives could be controlled in the air at the whim of the diver, as many believe possible, then diving would be a simple sport. A diver would never need to 'go over' or 'short' and certainly never land flat on his back. It is useless for a coach to admonish a diver for not 'pulling his head back' in order to save a back dive from going 'short'. The simple answer to this is that once you are in the air it is *too late* to do anything about it. Whether you are going to somersault at all, or whether you will have too little or too much rotation, is decided *before* your feet leave the board. Once you become airborne you are relatively helpless.

From a casual observation of a dive it does seem that many of the erroneous popular beliefs are correct, but unfortunately it is often a case of seeing what you want or expect to see. These beliefs are so often fallacies based on the results of optical illusion and wishful thinking; beliefs which can easily be shattered by a little practical experiment.

The Initiation of Rotation When the body is in flight it is a 'closed system' and no force within the system can cause it to rotate if it is not already rotating. To start a body rotating *two* opposing forces must be applied to the body. To be effective, these forces must be in opposition but their lines of action must not coincide, i.e. they must be off-set to form what is technically termed a 'couple' (Fig. 118).

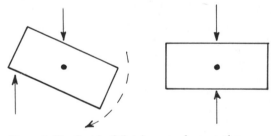

Fig. 118. The Couple. Offset forces produce rotation

During the flight of a dive there is only *one* force acting on the body, the force of gravity, so the diver is always balanced in the air. He cannot overbalance or set himself rotating (Fig. 119a).

In order to rotate, a diver must employ some other force. The only force available to him is the 'reaction' of the earth's surface. When he stands on the earth's surface, it is opposing the force of gravity acting downwards on his body. His muscular system keeps him upright. When standing too long, his muscles tire and he falls over, i.e. he overbalances.

The earth's surface reacts upwards in effect through his feet, and as he topples over, his centre of gravity passes outside the base (his feet). A couple is formed and he rotates through 90° from vertical to horizontal, i.e. 'falls flat on his face'. When this is performed from a diving board, the extra height will enable him to enter head first (Fig. 119b).

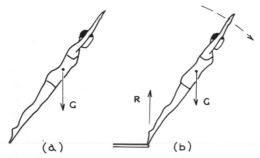

Fig. 119. The body is always balanced in the air, but easily overbalances on land

The body movements needed to provide the turning force necessary to produce the angular momentum required during the flight must be started whilst the feet are in contact with the board, that is during the take-off, and must be completed just *before* the feet lose contact with the board. A little experiment sitting on a swivel chair will prove this conclusively. It will not be possible to set the body rotating unless the feet are in contact with the floor. With the feet raised from the floor it will be found impossible to set the chair rotating.

When rotating in a swivel chair, it is not possible to stop the rotation by any action on the part of the performer. The only way in which the rotation can be stopped is by touching some 'external' object such as the wall or floor or something fixed to either.

Methods of Creating Angular Momentum (Producing the Turning Force)   There are basically four methods of producing angular momentum:

1. Overbalancing (Lean).
2. Momentum Transfer (Jerk).
3. Eccentric Leg Thrust (Hips Bent).
4. Eccentric Board Thrust (Springboard Only).

1. OVERBALANCING (LEAN)

This is the simplest method of creating rotation, especially for the beginner. Examples of dives performed entirely by this method are the elementary Sitting Dive, and the Pike Fall (Fig. 120), and the Armstand Back Fall, and the Dead Drop (Fig. 121).

Fig. 120. The Sitting Dive and Pike Fall

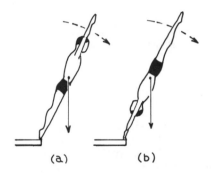

(a) (b)

Fig. 121. The Dead Drop and Armstand Back Fall

The Armstand Back Fall The diver overbalances by moving his centre of gravity forward beyond his point of support. His body pivoting about his hands rotates at an increasing rate, reaching a maximum at a position approximately 48° from the vertical, at which point his hands will lose effective purchase on the board. His body will then continue to rotate at the *same* angular velocity during the flight. When performed from the 10 metre board, the only way in which he can control his rate of rotation is to push away from the board early enough, i.e. before he reaches the 48° position of maximum velocity during the overbalancing (see Fig. 121b).

The Dead Drop When performing the Dead Drop, the diver will feel the acceleration as the body overbalances. As the body approaches the 48° position he will feel himself losing effective contact with the board and will instinctively start to extend his ankles to maintain contact.

The beginner will usually push away quickly when he feels this point approaching. It needs great control to keep the legs straight and still at this critical point (Fig. 122).

The downward force G can be resolved into the tangential force T (pulling away) and the 'reaction' force R (pressure on the feet).

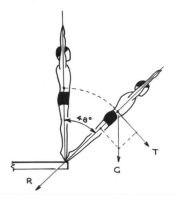

Fig. 122. The feet lose contact at 48° from the vertical

The body loses effective contact when the tangential force exceeds the reaction force. This position is reached at 48° from the vertical.

Lean not Necessary for Rotation All Forward and Back Dives require the body to overbalance just prior to the feet leaving the board. This is to ensure that the centre of gravity is set in motion *away* from the board for reasons of safety; once set in motion the centre of gravity will continue in motion at a constant rate in a horizontal direction during the flight (see Chapter 17). This slight lean at take-off will inevitably provide some angular momentum, and it is often stated that lean is a necessary requirement of somersaults, the amount of lean increasing with the number of somersaults to be performed. This statement is based on observations of what divers do instinctively instead of what they could do if better informed, for if lean were necessary to create rotation, Reverse and Inward Somersaults would not be possible.

The greater the lean at take-off the greater will be the angular momentum created, but only at the expense of height and therefore time. It should be reduced to a minimum consistent with the requirements of safety and aesthetics. Any lean during the take-off for a Reverse and Inward Dive will induce angular momentum in the wrong direction, which will need to be overcome by extra angular momentum in the correct direction if the dive is to be performed successfully. In these dives, lean is not required to ensure that the centre of gravity is set in motion away from the board, as this is provided for automatically if the respective take-offs are performed correctly.

Note: The angle of lean at take-off is that angle between the vertical and a line projected from the toes through the body's centre of gravity, irrespective of the position of the upper trunk (see Fig. 106 and Fig. 107).

2. MOMENTUM TRANSFER (Jerk)

When free in the air, an armswing will result in the trunk moving *towards* the arm; when the arm stops moving, the trunk stops. If the trunk is prevented from reacting, the momentum stored in the arm as a result of the armswing will be transferred to the rest of the body, pulling it round in the *same* direction. We say momentum from the 'part' has been transferred to the 'whole'.

For a given mass, the momentum stored in the 'part' of the body set in motion during the take-off will depend on the speed with which it is moving in the required direction at the moment the feet leave the board. The faster the 'part' is moving at the moment of take-off, the greater the amount of angular momentum stored in it. Double the speed produces twice the momentum. The angular momentum stored in the 'part' during this important phase of the take-off will be transferred to the whole during the flight, rotating it in the same direction.

As momentum = mass × velocity, a mass moved a short distance at high speed will produce more momentum than when moved a greater distance at a slower speed. As the initiation of rotation must be co-ordinated with the final leg drive at take-off, this becomes of vital importance, especially in multiple somersaulting dives.

Arm Transfer with the Swivel Chair   Transfer of momentum by an armswing can be demonstrated quite easily when sitting in a swivel chair. With the feet on the floor, an arm should be swung from the side extended position across in front of the body. Just as the arm completes its swing, the feet are raised from the floor. The chair will immediately commence rotating in the direction of the armswing. When this same action is performed with the feet off the floor, the chair will react by rotating *towards* the arm (see also Chapter 14, p. 147, Fig. 88).

Armswing Transfer – Backward Rotation   During the take-off for a Back or Reverse Dive, if the arms are swung vigorously forward, upward and backward, considerable angular momentum will be imparted to the arms. When the arms reach the limit of their movement in the shoulder joint, or are stopped by muscular action, the shoulders will be pulled back. If at this point the feet are losing contact with the board,

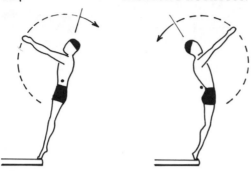

Fig. 123. Armswing transfer, backward rotation

the body will rotate about its centre of gravity with the angular momentum originally stored in the arms (Fig. 123).

Angular momentum, a product of moment of inertia and angular velocity, remains constant. As the moment of inertia of the arms about the shoulder joint is only approximately one-eighth that of the trunk about the centre of gravity, the trunk will rotate at only one-eighth the angular velocity of the arms.

Trunk Transfer for Backward Rotation   During the take-off for Back or Reverse Dives, the same effect can be produced to an even greater degree by 'jerking' the upper trunk, i.e. head and shoulders, backward at take-off. Momentum = mass × velocity, therefore more mass, greater momentum (Fig. 124). During the take-off, the trunk should be bent forward at the hips at the *start* of the leg drive. As the legs extend, the trunk is moved upwards and backwards. The back take-off is more efficient than the standing forward take-off, as the body movement is upwards. Compare Fig. 124 with Fig. 125.

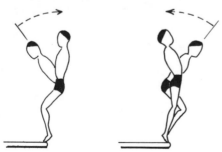

Fig. 124. Trunk transfer, backward rotation

This is why standing Front Somersaults are more difficult to execute correctly than Back Somersaults, especially when performed in the straight position.

Momentum transfer is the only method of obtaining angular momentum in reverse dives, all other methods being negative (providing angular momentum in the wrong direction).

Some divers believe that rotation in reverse dives is achieved by pushing *back* with the feet. Strain gauges have been fixed to the boards to register the actual force applied. Unfortunately this is muddled thinking. It is not possible to push *backwards* with the feet, one can only push downwards, the line of thrust being from the hip joint to the toes. Any force read on a strain gauge, is a measure of the *reaction* to the backward movement of the upper trunk head and arms. If the board was not there, i.e. in free fall, the feet would move backwards (see Fig. 86, page 145).

Trunk Transfer for Forward Rotation   With Forward and Inward Dives, the same principle applies, except that the upper trunk moves forwards instead of backwards. Transfer of momentum from the upper trunk in Forward and Inward Dives is obtained by moving the shoulders forward vigorously as the feet give their final push at take-off (Fig. 125). In practice, the farther we move the head and upper trunk away from the vertical, i.e. downward, the less height is obtained in the flight.

Fig. 125. Trunk transfer, forward rotation

During the take-off the trunk should be as near vertical as possible at the start of the leg drive. As the legs extend, the trunk is moved forward rather than downward. To prevent loss of height, the upper trunk should be moved vigorously through a *small* angle (jerk). Moving the trunk through a large angle will not only reduce height, but will take longer to execute, and will often reduce the power of the final leg drive by slowing it down. Moving the trunk quickly through a small angle will take less time and can be completed during the final phase of the leg drive without reducing its efficiency.

Armswing Transfer – Forward Rotation   With Forward and Inward Dives the normal upward armswing is in the wrong direction. When performing standing Forward Dives or Inward Dives from the firmboard, the diver should start with his arms stretched above his head. His arms will then swing forward at take-off in the same direction as the upper trunk, thereby giving combined transfer of momentum from the arms and upper trunk (Fig. 126).

Fig. 126. Armswing transfer, forward rotation

The springboard take-off presents special problems with these dives, as the arms normally swing forward and upward from the hips to assist in depressing the board. When the arms reach a position above the head, the direction of the armswing must be *reversed*. As the final thrust from the board is made with the feet, the arms must be swinging *forward* to enable transfer of momentum to be obtained from the armswing (Fig. 127).

Fig. 127. Directional armswing for Forward and Inward Dives

Observations on Momentum Transfer   In practice, momentum transfer from the arms can be combined with that of the upper trunk to provide a strong turning force when performing multiple somersaulting dives.

This is especially effective with back and reverse movements, as the normal upward armswing is in the same direction as the body rotation (see Fig. 123).

With Forward and Inward Dives this same advantage can be achieved, providing the armswing is made 'directional', i.e. changes direction when above the head (see Fig. 127).

3.   ECCENTRIC LEG THRUST (Hips Bent) (Fig. 128)

When the legs straighten at take-off, the thrust is along a line projected upwards from the toes passing through the hip joint. If the body is straight at take-off (a), so that this line passes through the body's centre of gravity as well as the hip joint, the body will rise, but there will be no rotation from this action. If, during the take-off for a Forward or Inward Dive, the body is bent forward at the hips (b) or (c), or the back is rounded so that the body's centre of gravity lies in front of the hip joint at the completion of the leg thrust, an off-centre or eccentric turning force will be applied, causing rotation of the body about its centre of gravity, in addition to the upward motion. The greater the distance between the hip joint and the centre of gravity, the greater will be the angular momentum created, but the less force there will be available to project the body upwards, and vice versa.

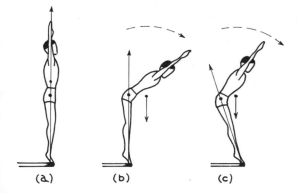

Fig. 128. Eccentric leg thrust

A little experiment with a billiard ball will prove this effectively. By striking the ball with the cue in line with the centre of the ball, the ball will be projected away, in line with the cue but with no lateral rotation (spin). When the ball is struck with the cue off-centre, the ball will travel in the same direction but will now have side spin (Fig. 129). It should be observed that although side spin is imparted to the ball, the path of its centre of gravity is unaltered.

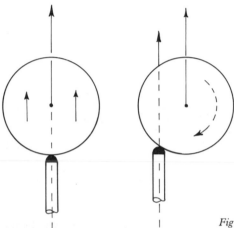

Fig. 129. Billiard ball experiment

On Forward and Inward Dives, eccentric leg thrust can easily be combined with method No. 2 (Momentum Transfer) to provide the additional angular momentum needed for multiple somersaults. In both methods No. 2 (Momentum Transfer) and No. 3 (Eccentric Leg Thrust), the amount of angular momentum imparted to the body varies in proportion to the force applied, i.e. twice the force applied, double the angular momentum created. This is in accordance with the second Law of Motion.

4. ECCENTRIC BOARD THRUST (SPRINGBOARD ONLY) (*Fig. 130*)

The line of thrust from the end of a rising springboard is at right angles to its surface. If at the moment of take-off, this line passes outside the body's centre of gravity, then a turning force will be imparted. In forward and backward take-offs (a), this will assist the general rotation of the body, but in Reverse and Inward Dives (b), it provides rotation in the wrong direction.

(a)   (b)   *Fig. 130. Eccentric board thrust*

N.B. As in method No. 3 (Eccentric Leg Thrust), the greater the distance between the body's centre of gravity and the line of action of the board thrust, the greater will be the angular momentum created, but the less force available to project the body upwards. On forward and backward take-offs this method is closely linked with method No. 1 (Overbalancing).

Summary of Methods Used

Method	*Diving Group to which Applicable*
1. Overbalancing	Forward, Back, Armstand Somersaults
2. Momentum Transfer	All groups
3. Eccentric Leg Thrust	Forward, Inward
4. Eccentric Springboard Thrust	Forward, Back

Diving Groups	*Method Applicable*
Forward Dives	Nos. 1, 2, 3, and 4
Back Dives	Nos. 1, 2, and 4
Reverse Dives	No. 2 only
Inward Dives	Nos. 2 and 3

19. *Control of Rotation in Flight*

All dives are somersaults consisting of either forward or backward rotation whilst travelling outward from the board during flight. The simple basic dives are half somersaults. During the flight the body rotates about an imaginary horizontal axis passing through its centre of gravity, and the body will always remain balanced about this point irrespective of any movement of the head, limbs or trunk.

The First Law of Motion states in effect that an object rotating will continue to rotate indefinitely until it is stopped by some external force. A diver somersaulting in the air will continue to somersault until he meets an external force, i.e. the water. In many dives it does seem that the diver stops his rotation when he stretches for his entry, but this is not so. There is a great deal of difference between what a diver does, and what he seems to do and also what he thinks he does.

The problem confronting the diver is, what control if any has he over the body's rotation during the flight? Can he speed up or slow his rotation? If it is not possible to *stop* the body rotating, what can he do to ensure a vertical entry? Unless he understands these problems and resolves them he will never progress far. This applies to the teacher and coach to an even greater degree. There is no substitute for personal experience, and the coach should avail himself of a swivel chair or turntable and prove these theories by practical experiment.

Practical Experiments Try the following experiment on the swivel chair or turntable. Set yourself rotating with your arms stretched sideways, then bring your arms in close to your body. You find as your arms come close to your body that you rotate faster, then as you stretch them out sideways again your rotation will slow down. Providing that the friction on your swivel chair or turntable is not too great, you can repeat this many times. Sit on the turntable and lean back, then, after setting yourself rotating, draw your knees into a tuck position, the result is even more startling. When you stretch your body, it seems to be 'resisting' the rotation, but nothing is destroyed because as you bring your knees up the original speed of rotation is resumed.

Conservation of Angular Momentum What you are demonstrating is the conservation of angular momentum. When a body is rotating about a particular axis, we say it is doing so by virtue of its angular momentum about that axis. Angular momentum is a measure of the amount of rotary motion possessed by a body. This angular momentum, rotational momentum, or somersaulting energy, call it what you will, was imparted to your body when force was applied against some external object to set you turning. The same applies to the diver. He can only set himself rotating by the aid of some external resisting object such as the bathside or diving board. The greater the force he uses to start his rotation at the take-off, the more angular momentum will his body possess during the flight. This angular momentum remains constant in the body and cannot be reduced, increased or destroyed by any action the diver may make during the flight.

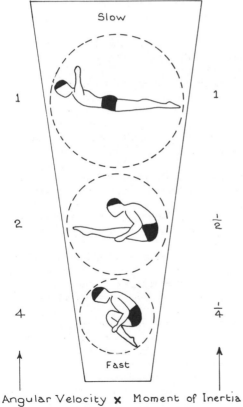

Angular Velocity **x** Moment of Inertia
= Angular Momentum

Fig. 131. The body position effects the rate of spin

Factors within our Control   The *angular momentum* present in a rotating body is a product of its angular velocity or rate of rotation and its moment of inertia or resistance to rotation. It follows that any increase in one must be compensated by a proportionate decrease in the other and vice versa. If the moment of inertia (resistance) is doubled then the angular velocity (spin) will be halved and if the moment of inertia is halved then the angular velocity will *automatically* double itself. The angular velocity is the rate of rotation of the body about its centre of gravity in a given direction, and providing the position is maintained unaltered it remains constant. You can begin to see why your body slowed down on the turntable when you stretched yourself, and speeded up again when you made yourself more compact. You were alternately increasing and decreasing your moment of inertia (Fig. 131).

Rotational Resistance   The *moment of inertia* of the body about its centre of gravity, is a measure of the amount of rotational inertia or resistance presented by the body to change in angular velocity. (Note: the word 'moment' in this instance has nothing to do with a moment of time.) Its effect on the rotation depends on the distribution of the body mass about the centre of gravity. The farther away the body mass is from the centre of gravity, the greater the moment of inertia and the greater the resistance to rotation. The nearer the body mass is to the centre of gravity, the smaller is the value of the moment of inertia and the less the resistance to rotation.

When you tie a weight on to the end of a length of string and swing it in a circle above your head, you will find that the shorter you keep the distance from the weight to your hand (the radius) the easier and faster it turns. As you let the string out, increasing the radius of the circle, the weight becomes harder to turn and slows down because you have increased its moment of inertia.

The distance of the body mass from its centre of rotation has a very great influence on its moment of inertia or resistance to rotation. In the case of the weight on the string the moment of inertia is found by multiplying the mass or weight by the square of the radius (see Fig. 79).

Moment of Inertia of the Body   In the case of the diver it becomes a little more difficult, because the various parts of the body are at different radii from his centre of gravity. Each part of the body has to be multiplied by the square of the radius, then added together to find the resultant moment of inertia for that particular body position. The accuracy of the result depends on the size of the body parts chosen. The smaller the size of each part, the more accurate the result. From our calculations we find that the moment of inertia of the body in the close pike position, is approximately half of what it is in the straight position, and in the compact tuck position it is approximately a quarter of that in the straight position (see Fig. 131, right-hand column).

The Effect of Change in Body Position   During the flight, the speed of the somersault can be controlled by alteration to the body position. The nearer the outer parts of the body are brought to the centre of rotation (centre of gravity), the less the resistance to turning and the faster the body will rotate, i.e. 'the tighter the tuck the faster the spin'. Likewise the farther away the parts of the body are moved from the centre of gravity the greater the resistance to turning and the slower the body will rotate.

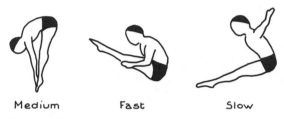

Medium   Fast   Slow

Fig. 132. The tighter the pike the faster the spin

A diver performing a Forward 2½ Somersault Pike from the 3 metre springboard should hold his legs just below the backs of the knees and pull into a close pike position with a round back to reduce his moment of inertia and so obtain the maximum spin. If he were performing a Forward 1½ Somersault Pike from 10 metres he would normally use the open pike position to increase his moment of inertia and so reduce his rate of spin (Fig. 132).

When a diver somersaults in the straight position, then closes into the pike position, his moment of inertia is halved and he automatically spins twice as fast. If he closed to a tuck position which could reduce his moment of inertia to a quarter, he would spin automatically four times as fast. If he then reverted to his straight position his angular velocity would return to its original rate. This occurs in flying somersaults (Fig. 133).

Control of the Dive during the Flight   During the flight, increasing and decreasing the body's moment of inertia by altering the relative position of parts of the body can play an important part in the control of the dive. In the Pike Dive, the body rotates faster as the pike position is assumed and then slows down as the body opens out for the entry.

Fig. 133. Flying 1½ *Somersault*

The fact that the angular velocity (rate of rotation) increases as the pike position is assumed, means that less angular momentum is needed for a dive performed in the pike position than for a similar dive in the straight position, as both require the same moment of rotation between take-off and entry. Therefore the body will always be rotating slower on entry from a pike dive than from the same dive performed in the straight position (angular velocity = angular momentum ÷ moment of inertia). The same remarks apply to dives performed in the tuck position to an even greater degree.

When a diver feels that he is not rotating fast enough during the flight, he can pull in tighter his pike or tuck position, and if necessary hold on to the position a little longer before opening out for entry. If the diver finds that he has obtained too much rotation at take-off, then he will show the position for only a brief moment, opening out much earlier to slow down his rotation to prevent the dive 'going over' on entry.

Difficulty with the Straight Position   There is very little means of control in dives performed in the straight position because there is little difference between the position in flight and the position at take-off. The only means of reducing the moment of inertia of the body about its somersaulting axis in the straight position during the flight is to hollow the back and/or lower the arms down sideways. When the arms are extended later above the head for entry the body's moment of inertia will be increased, thereby reducing its angular velocity. Divers with supple backs have considerable advantage over their less fortunate colleagues when performing Back or Reverse Dives in the straight position (Fig. 134). The majority of women divers are able to arch their

Fig. 134. A supple back is an advantage

backs to such an extent that for all practical purposes it resembles a 90° pike position (Fig. 134a). This could halve their moment of inertia enabling them both to rotate more slowly at entry and also to have extra control over their rotation during the flight.

This is extremely valuable in dives such as the Back and Reverse $1\frac{1}{2}$ Somersaults Straight. Not only does the extreme arch position require less angular momentum and give greater control at entry, it also allows the diver to spot the water early in the dive well before the legs reach the vertical position (compare (a) and (b) in Fig. 134).

Control of the Entry   For a given angular momentum, a diver rotates with a certain angular velocity dependent on the position he assumes during the flight. When he stretches for entry he will reduce his angular velocity to a minimum, *but he cannot stop himself rotating*, i.e. he cannot destroy his angular momentum. This fact must be allowed for by aiming for a slightly 'short' entry to prevent 'going over', or by employing some means of correction during the entry (see Chapter 21). For a given number of rotations (somersaults) a compact body position will require less angular momentum, and will therefore rotate slower when the body is stretched at entry.

Feet-first Entry Problems   The moment of inertia of the body about its centre of gravity with the arms stretched above the head is greater than with the arms by the sides. This is one reason why a head-first entry is easier to control than a feet-first entry with the hands by the sides. When a diver preparing for a feet-first entry feels that he may over-rotate, he will instinctively shoot his hands above his head to slow his rotation. He will hold this position for as long as possible before bringing his hands to his sides as required for a feet-first entry.

Conclusion   Whilst the limbs are moving, altering the body's moment of inertia the diver is able to control his rate of rotation within limits. When he stops moving his limbs, he rotates at a constant rate over which he has no control. This explains why the basic dives in the pike position are easy scoring dives. With the pike position there is *continuous* movement of the limbs into and out of the position. The diver is able to control his rate of rotation throughout the dive. The body in the extended straight position, once considered the basic position and easiest to control, is found to be the most difficult. This is why the degree of difficulty of the Forward Dive Straight has increased in value over a period of years.

20. *Spotting*

The subject of 'spotting' when rotating in the air has caused much heated discussion amongst coaches and performers of gymnastics, trampolining and diving. On the one hand there are those who believe that the performer *looks* for specific objects in order to know his position. Conversely there are those who believe that this is not possible, but rather that the performer somehow *knows* where he is instinctively. Most trampolinists favour the spotting viewpoint, while divers seem divided in their views, some believing in 'spotting', others in 'knowing'.

It is quite easy to see why trampolinists favour the spotting technique. The bed of a trampoline is a restricted area set above floor level. It is also a yielding landing medium, which can react by projecting the performer off at an angle so that he may miss the bed altogether when he finally lands. The gymnast's landing area is usually a mat on a firm gym floor. His main concern is to remain upright when he lands. The diver's landing area being water makes it more difficult to remain vertical, but less disastrous if he overthrows. The diver has less to worry about on entry as the landing is relatively 'softer'. The gymnast and trampolinist must maintain their balance when landing; if their eyes are closed while somersaulting they must regain visual awareness for the landing.

Visual Awareness The brain receives continuous information from the eyes, acting on that which is needed, while suppressing that which is of no immediate use. Anything that is important is stored in the memory and can be recalled when required. During the performance of any physical act, the eyes and brain working together constantly sift and check the visual impressions received to ensure that all is as it should be for the protection of the body. A performer who does not use his eyes fully is obviously at a disadvantage. Performers who use their eyes to the best advantage will be more relaxed and sure of themselves and less liable to become involved in accidents.

The gymnast and trampolinist *must* open the eyes in preparation for the landing. They are then able to assess quickly the correctness of the landing and make the necessary allowances to ensure their safety. The beginner diver has more latitude on entry into the water. It will not matter if he is short or past vertical, so he tends not to use his eyes unless he is instructed to. While this may not matter so much from the bathside or low boards, it becomes a serious matter when attempting dives from the higher boards because of the increased force of impact at entry.

Seeing and Balance at Take-off It is an easily verified fact that focusing the eyes on some object stabilizes the body and helps to maintain balance when standing or walking. One has only to shut the eyes to experience an immediate loss of balance control. As balance is so important during the take-off, divers should be taught to use their eyes from the very beginning. This visual awareness becomes more important as the difficulty of the dive increases. By its use divers acquire more confidence and gain a greater consistency of performance. The diver who learns to use his eyes at take-off will find the transfer from the basic to the more difficult dives easier to accomplish. This does not imply that the 'spotters' are right and the others wrong; far from it.

Spotting during Take-off During the take-off for standing Forward and Reverse Dives, the diver usually focuses his eyes on some point in front, at head level if possible. For back and inward take-offs, the diver usually focuses his eyes on the far end of the board. During the final phase of the leg drive the diver may change his focus point. On Back and Reverse Dives in the straight position, the eyes will usually change focus to a point overhead. On Inward Dives, the focus point may change to a point nearer the feet, and on Forward Dives the eyes may 'fix' on the entry point. With the running take-off, the eyes are usually focused on the front end of the board until the feet make contact. During the final leg drive the eyes may refocus to some other vantage point.

Spotting during the Flight Directly the diver loses contact with the board, the question of balance no longer applies. During the flight through the air the diver is always balanced about his centre of gravity. He will also be rotating about his centre of gravity and new problems arise. When somersaulting in the air, the performer has to decide at what moment to break from the flight position to effect an entry. There is not a great deal of latitude; he cannot afford to break too early or too late. Some performers are quite adamant that they look for some fixed point before deciding to break. Others are equally sure that this is impossible. They quote instances of divers keeping their eyes shut when rotating to prove their point.

Spotting during Twists The ballet dancer overcomes this problem during a pirouette by keeping the *head* fixed in space for as long as possible while the *body* is rotating. He focuses the eyes on one spot for as long as possible, then when the head is twisted on the spine as far as it will go, he turns his head rapidly in the general direction of rotation. He turns his head faster than the body is rotating and refocuses on the original spot. By use of this technique, he is able to re-establish visual awareness during the major part of each revolution and so maintain his balance.

Divers are able to use this technique during simple Twist Dives, such as the Back and Reverse Dives with $\frac{1}{2}$ Twist or the Forward Dive 1 Twist. During the Forward Dive with 1 Twist, the diver spots the water at take-off and maintains his forward head position until a quarter twist has been performed. During the next half twist he turns his head rapidly to enable him to refocus on the water again as quickly as possible.

Practical Experiments When making a first attempt at a new dive, the diver usually shuts his eyes as he leaves the board and hopes for the best. This is an instinctive reaction present with most first attempts. We call this first tentative attempt, a 'feeler'. The 'spotters' would say that if the diver used his eyes he would know where he was, and so would have no problems. Anyone with practical experience of this situation realizes that it is not so simple as the 'spotters' would have us believe. This can easily be proved by sitting on a swivel chair or turntable and spinning round slowly. It will be very difficult to focus on any particular object for any length of time. As the speed increases it will be found impossible to focus on any one object.

While the body is rotating, the brain receives a confused mixture of visual information from which nothing of value can be retained. The performer becomes completely disorientated and will usually find it more satisfactory to either keep the eyes out of focus or to close them under these conditions. The same applies when the body is rotating in the head-over-heels somersaulting plane – only to a greater extent.

The Beginner The human body was not designed to function upside-down and when placed in this position the beginner becomes completely disorientated. After a prolonged period of practice, however, the body will learn to adapt to even this unnatural position, so that instead of 'feeling lost' when upside-down, the brain re-establishes effective orientation, i.e. the diver knows where he is when upside-down during a somersault even though his eyes may be closed.

This phenomenon can be observed when the young beginner performs his first roll in from the side. When he surfaces he is confused. He does not know which way to turn and often commences to swim in the wrong direction. After a few more repetitions he will become aware of his position immediately he surfaces. It cannot be sight alone that enables an experienced diver to know where he is, otherwise the beginner would use it. It must be something that is acquired by practice.

Practical Experience Experience tells us that the ability to know when to break for the entry increases with the number of times we practise the dive. Therefore it cannot depend on sight. It is of little use to tell a diver at his first attempt to look for a specific point in order to know when to make the break. This is why a coach will give an 'out', so that the diver will *hear* and re-act accordingly. As the diver gets used to the dive, he starts to come out at the right moment automatically. The more practice he has the more accurate does his timing become.

When he breaks, his rate of rotation will be reduced considerably. He is then able to regain visual awareness, and focus his eyes on the entry point. Many divers think that they look for and spot the water, *before* making the decision to break. This is obviously not possible with a 'blind' dive such as the Back or Reverse $1\frac{1}{2}$ Somersault in which the diver cannot see the water until the actual entry. If sight cannot be relied on, there must be something other than sight which tells the performer at what precise moment to make the break. It is in the vestibular apparatus of the inner ear that we must look for the solution.

The Vestibular Senses   The vestibular mechanism of the inner ear consists of five chambers concerned with balance. Together they act as a sophisticated spirit-level sensing changes in bodily movement. The three semicircular canals are set at right angles to one another so that change of movement of the head in any direction can be detected and the brain informed.

The body rotates at a constant angular velocity about its centre of gravity during the flight. At the same time, the centre of gravity is tracing a parabolic flight path. As a result the head traces a cycloid path through the air (Fig. 135).

As the head rotates downwards in front of the flight path, it is moving in the same direction as the downward acceleration of the body due to gravity, and it therefore accelerates and overtakes the centre of gravity. When the head is rotating upwards behind the flight path it will be rotating in opposition to the downward gravitational pull and will decelerate, and be overtaken by the centre of gravity. This continual change of speed of the head during a somersault allows the brain to orientate itself during the flight.

After the diver has practised somersaulting, the brain associates the different *speeds* of the head with different *positions* of the body in space, i.e. we know when the head is in front of the flight path and when it is behind. Because the force of gravity acts in one direction only, i.e. downward, it is also possible for us to to know which way up we are at any time. Sensitive sense cells in two interconnected chambers register the position of the head at any given time. These two chambers (utricule and saccule) are concerned with balance and keep the brain informed of our position in relation to the vertical. The information fed to the brain from the vestibular apparatus of the inner ear when the body is rotating

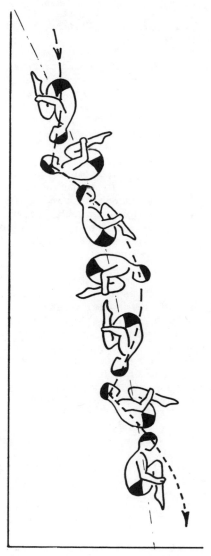

Fig. 135. The head traces a cycloid path

during a dive keeps us informed of our general position throughout the dive.

Awareness through Repetition   When a dive is repeated a number of times, the brain 'records' the sequence of movement as a 'memory pattern'. Eventually, the brain knows exactly where we are during the dive, and we perform the movement automatically. It is said to be 'stamped in'. When the required number of revolutions are completed, the diver automatically breaks from his position ready for the landing (entry). If he is asked to hang on to his position longer, in order to turn, for example, a Forward $1\frac{1}{2}$ Somersault into a Double Somersault, he would find it extremely difficult to accomplish at first. No matter how hard he tries to hang on, he would find himself automatically coming out at the $1\frac{1}{2}$ Somersault position.

During the first few attempts to increase the number of somersaults he would 'lose' himself. His brain not having experienced this particular movement, would have no memory to work on. As the repetitions increase, the brain begins to store the stimulus received from the senses and eventually sends out the right response to break for the entry, after the correct number of revolutions have been completed.

Continued practice brings greater consistency, as the information received by the brain is sifted and sorted until the correct pattern of movement is stamped in, never to be forgotten.

Physiology of Take-off   To perform even the simplest of somersaults, the diver should make full use of all the information received by the brain from every source available. During the take-off, he must establish and maintain visual awareness for as long as is possible. He must focus his eyes on some fixed point or points throughout the take-off phase. The visual information received, together with information received from the organs of balance in the inner ear, and that received from the postural muscles and joints, will ensure the accuracy of movement so essential at the take-off.

Physiology of Flight   During the flight, the mechanisms of the inner ear enable the trained diver to be aware of his general position in space. Although he is unable to focus his eyes on any specific object, he is usually able to re-orientate himself at each revolution, knowing approximately each time that he is the correct way up. A diver somersaulting in the air will usually keep his eyes closed or out of focus whilst rotating, only using them as he breaks from the flight position in preparation for the entry.

When rotating in the straight position, the head may remain relatively stationary in space during the major part of the flight with the feet

Fig. 136. The head remains 'fixed' in space

rotating 'about the head'. In such instances it may be possible to focus the eyes on various fixed objects during some part of this rotation (Fig. 136). When rotating in the compact tuck position during multiple somersaults the head is rotating too fast for this to be possible.

The Forward Break-out   When the dive has been learnt, the greatest problem is 'breaking-out' for the entry at the right moment. The 'break-out' must be early enough for the diver to establish visual awareness completely, so that he has time to prepare himself for the entry. Multiple somersaulting dives in the tuck position cause the greatest problems. Most experienced divers make the preparations to break early in the last somersault, in order to regain visual awareness for the entry. With dives such as the Forward $3\frac{1}{2}$ Somersault Tuck, or Inward $2\frac{1}{2}$ Somersault Tuck, the diver will change from the tuck to the pike position when in the head-up position at the last somersault, before he is in sight of the water. This will slow his rotation reducing it by a half (Fig. 137).

As he rotates forward, he will spot the water and be able to make the necessary adjustments to effect a vertical entry. As he opens out from the pike position, he will be able to keep the entry point in view until the moment of impact. (See also Chapter 21 'Entry Techniques', p. 210.)

The Backward Break-out   With the blind dives, such as the Back and Reverse $2\frac{1}{2}$ Somersaults Tuck, the break-out starts when the body is in the head-up position at the double somersault (Fig. 138). The diver

Fig. 137. The Forward Break-out   *Fig. 138. The Backward Break-out*

will change from the tuck to the pike position, so slowing his rotation. He will then sight the board and start to open out from the pike position making adjustments as necessary. He will change his focus point to the water at the appropriate moment. As he cannot sight the water until the last moment, these dives are usually entered slightly short (see Chapter 21, p. 210).

21. *Entry Techniques*

Advice given to early divers regarding entry technique sounds strange today. In a publication entitled *How to Dive* issued about the year 1910, it states: 'When diving from a low board you should strike the water at an angle of 45° with the back hollowed. The dive looks very elegant; especially if the tips of the fingers appear out of the water before the feet have entered it. As soon as the body is under the water, the back should be strongly hollowed and the legs bent back a little, so that you rise immediately to the surface.' In those days, the dive was not considered finished until the diver resurfaced. No attempt was made to enter vertically or go deep. The aim was to perform a graceful curve beneath the surface.

Entry Requirements   In competitive diving today, the entry into the water must in all cases be vertical, or nearly so, with the body straight and toes pointed. The dive is considered to be finished when the whole body is completely under the surface of the water.

The entry plays a very important part in the final assessment of a dive. It is indicative of the amount of control the performer has over the dive. One has only to attend any public display of diving to appreciate this fact. No matter how complicated and well executed the dive, there is silence until the entry. If the entry is near vertical, it brings forward a roar of approval. If it goes over, there is only a groan from the audience. As the vertical entry obviously plays such an important part in the dive, the question poses itself, what can a diver do, if anything, to achieve this elusive ideal?

Entry Problems   The most important factor affecting all entries is that the body is still rotating when it strikes the water. Whatever the diver does he cannot *stop* his body rotating. But he can *reduce* the rate of rotation to a minimum by stretching his body to its maximum just prior to the entry.

During the flight, the body rotates about its centre of gravity (Fig. 139a). Directly the surface of the water is broken at entry, the hands (or feet) are held, and become the axis of rotation (Fig. 139b). As the moment of inertia about this new axis is greater because of the increased distance of the body parts from it, the body rotation will be reduced to about one-third. The diver can employ various techniques to give the *effect* of stopping either his trunk or legs, but he cannot eliminate rotation entirely from the entry.

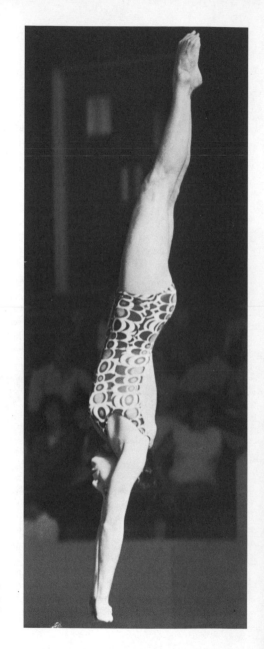

Plate 27.
Beverley Williams *(G.B.)*
European Youth
Highboard Champion
1973, displaying a perfect
line prior to entry

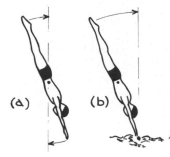

(a) (b)

Fig. 139. The body rotation is reduced on entry

Neither can a diver drop vertically. His centre of gravity follows a parabolic flight trajectory moving away from the board at a constant velocity throughout the dive. It may *seem* in certain dives that the body descends in a vertical line. During some part of a dive, the head may in fact do so, but the body as a whole cannot.

Types of Entry   There are only two methods of entering the water: head first and feet first. These entries can be from forward rotating dives, backward rotating dives, or from dives with no rotation (i.e. jump entries or the entry from an armstand dive). This results in six different types of entry.

1. Head-first with Forward Rotation (Forward and Inward Dives).
2. Head-first with Backward Rotation (Back and Reverse Dives).
3. Head-first with no Rotation (Armstand Dive).
4. Feet-first with Forward Rotation (Forward and Inward Dives).
5. Feet-first with Backward Rotation (Back and Reverse Dives).
6. Feet-first with no Rotation (Jumps).

These are all entirely different in their requirements, and also in the actual 'feel' of the entry.

Head-first Entries (Forward Rotation)   The forward rotating head-first entries (Forward and Inward groups) are the easiest entries to control as the entry point can be spotted early in the dive, usually at the same moment as the 'break' from the flight position is made (see Fig. 137). With the basic dives in these two groups performed in all three positions, the entry point can be held in focus for most of the dive (see Figs. 60 to 62 and Figs. 69 to 71). The Forward group has the advantage that the entry angle is identical to the flight line and the trunk follows the line of flight into the water slightly short of vertical. In the Inward group, the body is rotating 'against' the line of flight and so can never line up with it exactly unless the dive goes over slightly. An Inward Dive slightly over is much more acceptable for this reason than a Forward Dive slightly over would be.

Head-first Entries (Backward Rotation)   The backward rotating head-first entries (Back and Reverse groups) are 'blind' dives because the entry point cannot be seen until very late in the dive (see Fig. 138). Correct entries are more difficult to achieve because the diver usually has to break from his flight position well before he sees the water. For this reason these entries are always played short (see Figs. 63 to 68). The Back group has the advantage that, like the Forward group, the entry angle is along the flight line, whereas in the Reverse group the body is rotating 'against' the flight line.

Head-first Entry (No Rotation)   The armstand dive is the only head-first entry dive with no rotation. The diver must ensure that there is no rotation at take-off because there is very little he can do to reduce any unwanted rotation at entry.

Feet-first Entries (General)   It is more difficult to enter vertically from a feet-first dive than it is from a head-first dive. This is because the extended arm position in head-first entries increases the body's moment of inertia (resistance to rotation) to a greater amount than is possible with the arms by sides requirement for feet-first entries. For this reason, for a given amount of angular momentum, an entry with the arms by the sides will always rotate faster than if the arms are above the head. If the arms are extended above the head when approaching the water for a feet-first entry, it becomes easier to control.

Feet-first Entries (Forward Rotation)   Feet-first entries from the Forward group have the advantage that the trunk follows the line of flight. With the Inward group, the body is rotating 'against' the line of flight, so the trunk can never line up with it exactly unless the dive goes over slightly. As with head-first entries from the Inward group this is more acceptable than from the Forward group.

Feet-first Entries (Backward Rotation)   With backward rotating feet-first entries, it is possible to focus on the water very early (see Fig. 136). With feet-first entries from the Back group the body is rotating 'with' the flight line and it is easier to keep the legs near vertical at entry. With feet-first entries from the Reverse group, the body is rotating 'against' the flight line, so the legs cannot line up with it unless the entry goes over slightly.

Jumps   Feet-first entries from the Jumps are deceptively simple.

There should be no rotation in a jump, so any slight rotation either forward or backward will be very difficult to control.

Jumps in the tuck position are more difficult than straight jumps. If there is any trace of rotation at take-off it will increase rapidly directly the tuck position is assumed. Jumps in the pike position come half-way between in difficulty.

Body Alignment – Head-first Entries *(Fig. 140)*   There are two accepted methods of aligning the body at entry. For forward rotating head-first entries the Straight Entry Alignment position with the body perfectly straight is used. The chin is tucked in and abdomen drawn in. A very slight bend at the hips is sometimes employed with advantage (a). For backward rotating head-first entries the Arched Entry Alignment position, with the back arched slightly and the abdomen held flat, is used. The arms are extended backwards with the head between the arms, eyes focused on the entry point (b).

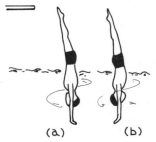

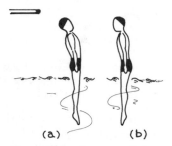

Fig. 140. Head-first entry alignment   *Fig. 141. Feet-first entry alignment*

Body Alignment – Feet-first Entries *(Fig. 141)*   Similar techniques are used for the feet-first entries. For forward rotating feet-first entries, the diver aims to enter slightly short in the Arched Entry Alignment position. This brings his feet under his hips and allows his legs to enter vertically followed by the trunk (a). For backward rotating feet-first entries the Straight Entry Alignment position often with a very slight bend at the hips is used. This allows the legs to enter vertically followed by the trunk (b).

Governing Factors   The more angular momentum required in a dive, the faster the body will be rotating at entry, and the more difficult it will be to effect a vertical entry. The angular momentum needed during a particular dive depends on the number of somersaults required, the position in which the somersaults are to be performed, and the time available. The greater the number of somersaults required during a dive, the more angular momentum needed. The more compact the body position during the somersault, the less angular momentum needed. The more height obtained from the take-off, the more time available during the flight, and less angular momentum needed.

For a given dive, the greater the height a diver can obtain from his take-off, the slower will he need to rotate during the flight, and the more control will he have at entry.

Control of the Entry When he stretches for entry a diver will reduce his angular velocity to a minimum but he cannot stop himself rotating, i.e. he cannot destroy his angular momentum. This fact must be allowed for by aiming for a slightly 'short' entry to prevent 'going over', or by employing some means of correction during the entry. A diver rotating in the straight position will not be able to reduce his rotation very much on entry, and it is therefore more difficult to obtain a vertical entry from a dive in the straight position than from a dive performed in the pike or tuck position. A diver rotating in the pike position will reduce his rate of rotation by a half when he stretches for entry. If he was rotating in the tuck position his rate of rotation could be reduced to a quarter on entry.

Pike Control of Entry (Forward Rotation) Dives performed in the pike position have an additional means of control. As the body opens out for entry from Forward or Inward Pike Dives, the shoulders will be rotating in opposition to the general rotation of the body, and if it is performed correctly, they will remain fixed with reference to the vertical (see Figs. 60 and 69).

In fast rotating dives such as the Forward $3\frac{1}{2}$ Somersault Tuck, and Inward $2\frac{1}{2}$ Somersault Tuck, it is the usual practice to come out of the Tuck into a pike position just prior to entry in order to gain this additional control.

As the diver rotates into the last somersault of a '$3\frac{1}{2}$' he will be facing forward. He then shoots his legs out straight into the pike position, which immediately slows his rotation. He spots the entry position, and opens out at such a rate that his head follows the line of flight to the water (see Fig. 137).

Pike Control of Entry (Backward Rotation) A similar effect is seen with the legs in Back and Reverse Pike dives. As the body opens out for the entry the legs will be rotating in opposition to the general rotation of the body, and if performed correctly the legs will remain stationary with reference to the vertical (see Figs. 63 and 66).

In fast rotating dives such as the Back and Reverse $2\frac{1}{2}$ Somersault Tuck, it is preferable to straighten the legs into the pike position on the last somersault to reduce the speed of rotation. This gives the diver time to spot his position (usually the board). He then opens out at such a rate that his legs remain a little short of vertical for the entry (see Fig. 138).

The Vertical Entry Entries should always be aimed a little short of vertical. About 80° to the surface is a good angle for most dives. For slow rotating dives this can be increased to 85°. As the body is rotating at entry in all dives, every attempt must be made to avoid going past vertical. A dive going over is out of control, and very little can be done to rescue it.

If the body is at the correct approach angle as the fingers touch the water, the legs will reach the vertical position as the trunk submerges. Once the trunk is submerged, the water will absorb a great deal of the rotation (angular momentum). Various techniques can then be used under water when necessary to prevent the legs going past the vertical. By use of these underwater correcting techniques, it is possible on the basic dives in the Forward and Inward group to allow the body to be vertical as the fingers touch. If such entries were held straight, the legs would go over slightly, but by piking the body under water the legs remain vertical (see Fig. 142).

Underwater Technique Over the years, dives have increased in complexity, and the number of somersaults included have risen. Divers today are expected to perform the $2\frac{1}{2}$ Back, Inward, and Reverse Somersaults and the Forward $3\frac{1}{2}$ Somersault. This presents increasing problems at entry due to the high angular momentum stored in the body with these dives. When the body is finally stretched for the entry, there is still considerable spin to be dealt with.

Various underwater techniques, which have come to be known as 'saves', have evolved to overcome the problem of overthrowing at entry with these dives. The basic principle is to allow the body to continue to turn underwater in the direction of rotation of the dive. Although 'saves' can be used to prevent bad dives from becoming worse, this is not their intention. The 'save' is an underwater technique that is a necessary part of modern diving. It should only be used after divers have been taught a good stretched entry technique.

Evolution of the Save Saves have been used instinctively by top divers for a number of years. At first they were confined mostly to back and reverse entries which, being 'blind', were usually played short. The back save was used by Pete Desjardins very successfully in the thirties. It was during the fifties, especially at the 1952 and 1956 Olympics, that saving techniques were so ably demonstrated by such legendary U.S.A. divers as Bruce Harlan, Sammy Lee, Skippy Browning and Robert

Clotworthy. Unfortunately, divers at home started to practise the various saves, often starting them above the water, with hilarious results.

It is now generally accepted that the straight-line entry technique should be used with all dives in the learning stage, aiming for the bottom of the pool. Then the various correcting techniques can be employed as needed to attain the desired vertical entry.

The saves are of two main types. Firstly, saves used to pull a short dive into line, usually Back or Reverse dives, and secondly, saves used to prevent fast rotating dives with high angular momentum, such as the Forward $3\frac{1}{2}$ Somersaults, from overthrowing on entry.

Six types of save have evolved as follows:

Type of Save	Dive Group	Rotation Fast/Slow	Entry Over/Short
Front Pike Save	Forward/Inward	fast/slow	over
Front Roll Save	Forward/Inward	fast	short
Front Reaction Save	Forward/Inward	slow	short
Back Arch Save	Back/Reverse	fast/slow	short
Back Arch Bent Knee Save	Back/Reverse	fast	over
Back Knee Save	Back/Reverse	slow	over

Front Pike Save (*Fig. 142 and Fig. 143*)   The Front Pike Save, sometimes called the Front Somersault Save, can be employed on any forward rotating dive (Forward or Inward groups). Depending on how

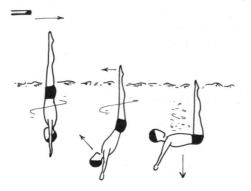

Fig. 142. Front Pike Save (slow rotating dives)

it is performed, it can be used on fast or slow rotating dives to obtain a vertical entry.

For slow rotating dives, such as the Forward or Inward basic dives, the diver aims to enter vertically. As the hips submerge, the arms are pressed out sideways, the head is ducked forward and the body bends at the hips into the open pike position. The body will normally remain in this position, back horizontal, until the downward momentum is absorbed (Fig. 142). The speed of the piking is such that the legs rotate in opposition to the general rotation of the body, resulting in the legs remaining vertical until submerged. If the body entered vertically and remained straight, the legs would go past vertical.

For fast rotating multiple somersault dives, the piking movement is the same, only performed much faster and usually with a closer pike position. Only experience will tell the diver when, how fast, and how close to pike (Fig. 143).

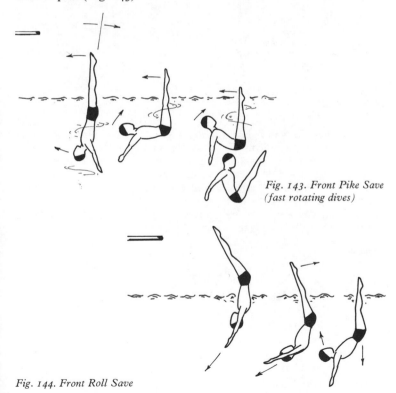

Fig. 143. Front Pike Save
(fast rotating dives)

Fig. 144. Front Roll Save

Front Roll Save (*Fig. 144*)   The Front Roll Save can be employed on fast forward rotating dives (Forward or Inward groups) entering short. The body enters in a slight pike position, trunk vertical. The pike position is held and the body allowed to continue rotating underwater. The body should be piked at entry sufficiently to get the trunk in as near vertically as possible.

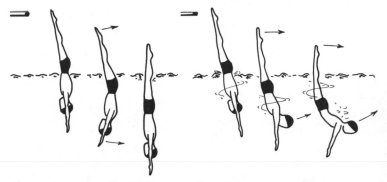

Fig. 145. Front Reaction Save
(pike entry)

Fig. 146. Front Reaction Save
(straight entry)

Front Reaction Save (*Fig. 145 and Fig. 146*)   The Front Reaction Save can be employed on slow forward rotating dives (Forward and Inward groups) entering short. The body enters in a slight pike position, if possible with the trunk near to vertical. When the trunk is submerged to the hips the body is straightened bringing the legs to the vertical position (Fig. 145). If the body is short but *straight* on entry, the back can be arched as the hips submerge, bringing the legs to a vertical position. The principle is the same (Fig. 146).

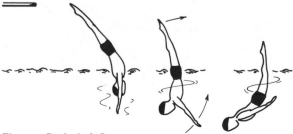

Fig. 147. Back Arch Save

Back Arch Save (*Fig. 147*)   The Back Arch Save can be employed on any back rotating dive (Back or Reverse groups) that is short on entry. As the diver enters the water in the arched position he pulls his arms down vigorously in front of his body from the overhead position to his thighs. At the same time he presses his head back and increases his body arch. This has the effect of pulling the legs into the vertical position. This is the 'original' save. It has been used instinctively by experienced divers for many years.

Back Arch Bent Knee Save (*Fig. 148*)   This save, sometimes called the Scoop and Bend Knee Save, can be employed on any back rotating dive with high angular momentum, such as the Back or Reverse 2½ Somersault, when there is danger of going over on entry.

It is very similar to the Back Arch Save, except that it is performed more vigorously, and the legs bend at the knees, as the knees submerge. This is a difficult save to perform successfully and is for the experienced diver only.

Fig. 148. Back Arch Bent Knee Save   *Fig. 149. Back Knee Save*

Back Knee Save (*Fig. 149*)   The Back Knee Save can be employed on any slow back rotating dive entering vertically to prevent it going over. The body is aligned for a straight entry, but as the knees reach the surface, they are drawn quickly through the water to the chest while maintaining the stretch to the bottom. The action of bending the knees pulls the lower legs back towards the vertical above the surface. The thighs, being horizontal, create a low pressure area behind them and prevent the displaced water rising, so avoiding splash.

The Splashless Entry   Although splash at entry should not be taken into account when evaluating a dive, it does make a difference to the final assessment. A splashless entry is now regarded as the hallmark of the expert. One would assume that the streamlined body position would be the ideal, but in practice it is found difficult to avoid splash with this type of entry. Many divers in the U.S.A. at one period used the Armstand cut-through as their first dive from the 10 metre platform. It was found by accident that if the feet were flattened immediately the toes entered the water, the water would 'bubble' at the surface but there would be no splash.

This led to similar experiments with head-first entries with the same result. It was found that if the hands were bent back at the wrists on entry there was the same characteristic bubbling entry and no splash. From the 3 metre springboard, divers often bend the hands back and spread the fingers, especially on back and reverse entries. From the 10 metre platform it is usual to clasp the hands interlocking the thumbs, one hand clamped over the other, palms forward. This flat-hand entry technique should be taught from the beginning, as the hands are then in the correct position for contact with the bottom. It also gives time for the hands to acquire the strength necessary to hold the position ready for later entries from heights.

Flat-hand Entry Technique   Just before the entry the hands are brought together, bent back at the wrists, one hand clamped over the other, thumbs interlocked, palms facing the water (see Fig. 8). As the hands make contact with the water the head is moved into line with the trunk, arms squeezing the ears. The low pressure area behind the hands provides a 'cushion' for the head, and no smack is felt on the head on contact with the water. While this may be of little consequence when diving from the side, it becomes of increasing importance from the higher boards.

The flat-hand technique also prevents the hands being deflected from the projected line of descent, and affords greater protection for the head in shallow water. Subject to the requirements of any 'saving' technique employed, the hands should be held clasped together until the body is completely submerged. The suction created by the hands causes resistance to the body's descent and aids in absorbing the downward momentum.

Entry Practice   The Pike Fall (Fig. 24) is used by competent divers from all heights in order to perfect this entry technique. When diving from the lower boards, up to heights of 3 metres, experienced divers often keep the hands bent back at the wrists but not clasped together.

This creates a greater suction area behind the hands and makes for even less disturbance at entry. It is very similar in effect to the feet-first entry. From the higher boards, the increased velocity at entry makes it difficult to maintain this separated hand position. From the higher boards, especially when diving from the 10 metre platform, it becomes necessary to clasp the hands together.

The velocity at entry from the 10 metre board is about 33 m.p.h. (53 km.p.h.) and it requires considerable strength in the shoulder girdle, arms and wrists to maintain the entry position. This entry alignment cannot be learnt overnight. It requires practice to provide time for the body to adapt itself to cope with these conditions.

The Pike Fall eliminates the complexities of the dive, allowing the diver to concentrate solely on the entry technique. Through experiment he will discover the technique which suits him best for different dives, and from each height of board.

Entry Analysis When a streamlined shape enters the water, the water is pushed aside and forced upwards (behind the object), eventually shooting up through the surface. When a non-streamlined shape enters the water, a low pressure mixture of air and water is created behind the object and the water that is pushed aside flows easily into this low pressure area instead of shooting to the surface.

An entry with flattened hands creates a low pressure area immediately behind the hands. This can easily be seen underwater in the form of a mass of air bubbles extending from behind the hands. A Front Pike Save will create the same effect to an even greater degree. At the completion of the pike roll the diver's back is horizontal providing a large low pressure area above the front of the trunk. All that is seen on the surface is a boiling effect, but no splash (see Fig. 142).

It is found that divers with broad shoulders, large chests and slim hips and legs have the ideal shape to produce splashless entries. The broad shoulders create a low pressure area around the waist and legs, keeping the displaced water below the surface.

22. *Twist Techniques*

Any dive in which the body rotates laterally about its long axis in addition to the forward or backward rotation is called a 'twist dive'. The ability of the diver and the trampolinist to execute rapid rotation about the twist axis whilst performing forward or backward rotation about the somersaulting axis has fascinated students of these sports for many years. It seems unbelievable that a person may be an expert at these highly complex movements yet may not be able to explain how he does them. The answer lies in the fact that an animal, particularly the cat, can be dropped upside down, yet will right itself and land safely on its feet. This implies that the movement is instinctive and not learnt.

During experimentation, it will be discovered that there are many different ways in which one may turn about the twist axis, each giving a different feeling. Some methods are easily performed by the beginner, but others may require a certain natural ability in order to execute correctly. As with somersaulting, the creation of twist is more complex than the average diver and coach are led to believe. To the uninformed it is simply a matter of turning the head in the direction in which it is desired to twist, and the body will follow. For rapid multiple twists the diver is usually advised to swing an arm vigorously across in front of the body, i.e. to 'wrap it up', and the body will twist in the same direction.

A study of divers on film seems at first glance to confirm this, but experiments on the swivel chair or turntable prove that in fact the body will 'twist' in the *opposite* direction to the armswing, and then only while the arm is moving. In practice the 'wrapping up' technique will, if performed *correctly*, provide the body tilt necessary to produce twist, but the arm action itself cannot produce twist unless the body is already somersaulting, as we shall see.

Methods of Creating Twist   There are basically four methods of achieving twist in dives, each producing an entirely different form of twist.

Some dives require one method of twist, some another. Other dives may require a combination of methods for their correct execution. These methods can be summarized as follows:

1. Twist from the Board (Momentum Transfer)
2. Arm Reaction Twist (Action-Reaction)
3. Cat Twist (Action-Reaction)
4. Body Tilt Twist (Somersault Transfer)

1. TWIST FROM THE BOARD

The simplest method and one used instinctively by the beginner is to take the twist from the board. This can be demonstrated quite easily with a jump from the bathside.

The technique used is that of momentum transfer as used to initiate rotation in somersaults. It is used chiefly in the Forward Dive $\frac{1}{2}$ Twist Straight (see Fig. 72).

Momentum Transfer Twist by transfer of momentum takes the form of a *continuous* rotation of the whole body about the long axis lasting throughout the flight (a side-rolling action). It is achieved by starting the upper trunk twisting during the take-off, i.e. whilst the feet are in contact with the board, usually by turning the shoulders about the long axis as the feet give their final push.

When the feet leave the board the momentum stored in the upper body will be transferred to the whole, and it will rotate in the original direction of rotation of the shoulders. The body will continue to rotate (twist) about its long axis throughout the flight without any further effort on the diver's part. He can control the rate at which he 'twists', i.e. his angular velocity about the long axis, by altering his moment of inertia about that axis, but he cannot stop himself 'twisting'.

Momentum Transfer in Practice What has been said concerning rotation about the somersaulting axis is equally true for rotation about the long axis of the body. When a diver takes his twist from the board during a Forward Dive $\frac{1}{2}$ Twist Straight, he will have angular momentum about his long axis as well as his somersaulting axis. If he has his arms extended sideways, his moment of inertia about his long axis will be at its greatest. When he closes his arms together above his head for the entry, his moment of inertia will be reduced by approximately one-third and his angular velocity about his long axis will be increased threefold, i.e. he will 'twist' three times as fast and he must allow for this if he is to effect a 'square' entry. The angular momentum about the twist axis remains constant.

Because twist by this method cannot be stopped during the flight, its use is usually confined to the basic headers with a half twist. It is extremely difficult to effect a square entry if a full twist is taken from the board. At one period the competitive rules stated that 'twist must not be taken from the board'. As an understanding of twisting developed, it was eventually altered to read 'twist must not *manifestly* be taken from the board'.

2. ARM REACTION TWIST

One or both arms may be used during the flight to cause the body to 'twist' through a small angle, or if repeated, through a larger angle, depending on the requirements of the dive being performed. These techniques are also used to square the body for the entry in twisting dives.

(a) *Using an Arm to Rotate the Trunk.* When an outstretched arm is swung across in front of the body which is in the straight position, the body will react by turning towards the arm, the pivot being the shoulder joint. The angular distance through which the arm turns in relation to that of the body will depend on their respective moments of inertia about the shoulder joint. The trunk will usually rotate through approximately 30° and the arm 90°. The arm can then be lowered in front of the body and raised sideways again passing through a neutral plane ready to repeated the process if necessary (see Fig. 88, page 147).

This technique is sometimes used to create twist in a Reverse Dive $\frac{1}{2}$ Twist Straight and Back Dive $\frac{1}{2}$ Twist Straight and is often used to square the body for entry in a Forward Dive 1 Twist Straight.

(b) *Using Both Arms to Rotate the Hips and Legs.* When the body is in the straight position and both arms are extended sideways the hips and legs can be rotated about the long axis of the body. The arms and shoulders will rotate in the opposite direction but owing to the greater moment of inertia of the extended arms and upper trunk about the long axis, the hips and legs will rotate in the required direction through a much greater angular distance than the arms and shoulders will in the opposite direction. The actual rotation occurs in the spine. The technique is often used at the completion of the twist in the majority of twisting somersault dives, to bring the hips and legs into line with the upper trunk just prior to entry.

3. CAT TWIST

The third method, as used by the cat when dropped from a height, is basically a *reaction* twist and is performed instinctively by anyone with natural ability. This method of twisting is entirely different in feeling and application to the method of taking twist from the board. This technique is used in the Forward and Inward Dives Piked with $\frac{1}{2}$ Twist, the Forward Dive Straight with 1 Twist and the Back and Reverse Dives Straight with $\frac{1}{2}$ Twist (see Fig. 53 and Fig. 73).

The competitive regulations require that: 'In pike dives with twist,

the twist must not be started until there has been a marked pike position.'
And: 'In straight dives with one half or full twist, the twisting must not
manifestly be done from the board.' It is not possible to use the Body
Tilt technique as there is insufficient angular momentum about the
somersault axis for it to be effective. This leaves the Cat Twist technique
as the only method available.

Cat Twist Technique   The Cat Twist is achieved by muscular action
during the flight and continues only for as long as the muscular action
continues. It can be demonstrated quite easily during a jump, providing
the body is bent at the hips or arched prior to starting the twist. It is a
very difficult technique to explain simply, but in practice the shoulders
are twisted followed by the hips and legs. Whilst the shoulders are
twisting about the spinal axis, the legs are circling in a conical manner
about the longitudinal axis in the opposite direction as in the Log Roll
described later. The twist is achieved by *decreasing* the moment of
inertia of the part being 'twisted' whilst *increasing* that of the part moving
in the opposite direction.

(a) *Using the Legs to Rotate the Upper Trunk*. If the body is bent at the
hips or the back rounded (front arch position) the upper trunk can be
rotated about the upper *spinal* axis. During this rotation the extended
legs and the hips will rotate in the opposite direction but owing to the
increased moment of inertia of the legs about the upper spinal axis, the
upper trunk will rotate in the required direction through a greater
angular distance than the legs will in the opposite direction (see Fig. 94).

This method is used usually at the start of the twist in Forward
Somersault with Twist Dives (twisting out of the pike). A similar effect
can be achieved by starting the twist from an arched back position as
would be used for all Back and Reverse Twist Dives, the axis of twist
being in the upper spine as before.

(b) *Using the Upper Trunk to Rotate the Hips and Legs*. If a twist is
started from the hips bent (or arched back) position as described above,
it is only possible to twist the upper trunk through an angle of approximately 50°. At this point, however, the hips and legs can be rotated in
the direction of the twist, about an axis through the lower half of the
spine. As the spine would be arched, the upper trunk would have an
increased moment of inertia about this lower spinal axis, so would be
prevented from reacting too far in the opposite direction. The body
would pass through a side arch position into a back arch (or hips bent)
position and the whole series of movements repeated if necessary.

Shoulder and Hip Twist   By keeping the spine arched forwards,
backwards and sideways, the upper trunk can be twisted about the hips

and legs (the axis of twist being in the upper spine) and the hips and legs can be twisted about the upper trunk (the axis of twist being in the lower spine). This movement can be performed continuously by a skilled diver. As this method of reaction twisting originates during the flight it can only be continued by repeated muscular action and can therefore be stopped at will, thus when using this method there is no danger of over twisting (see Fig. 94, page 149).

Brian Phelps's Demonstrations Brian Phelps demonstrated the Cat Twist technique on many occasions by twisting in the air at a call given *after* he had left the board. He also succeeded in imitating a cat by hanging on to the 5 metre board in an inverted pike position. After releasing his hold he would execute a complete half twist to land on all fours. He eventually became so adept at this form of twisting that he would drop from the 10 metre board feet first, and perform a half twist to the right followed by a half twist to the left before entering the water, feet first.

The Log Roll A practical example of this that can be attempted by anyone is the 'log roll' performed lying on the surface of the water with the body 'curved' slightly (Fig. 150). Viewing the performer end on, it will be seen that when the body is twisting in an anti-clockwise direction, hips and feet will be describing circles in the *opposite* direction. The angular momentum of the body about the spinal axis in the direction of twist will always be equal to the angular momentum of the hands, hips and feet about the longitudinal axis in the opposite direction. The net angular momentum will therefore always be zero.

Fig. 150. The Log Roll

Essential Features of the Cat Twist The essential feature of a Cat Twist is that the body must *not* be straight. It must be bent or curved in some way either forwards, sideways, or backwards throughout the movement. The body will continue to twist only for as long as the muscular action continues; therefore when incorporated into a dive there is no danger of overtwisting on entry. An essential requirement is a supple spine as the twist axis is in the spine.

4. BODY TILT TWIST

After a period of experimenting a diver will discover that it is easier to twist when the body is somersaulting than when it is not. It is very difficult to perform more than one twist during a jump, but relatively easy to perform a double twist during a somersault. If the proviso is made that the twist must not be started from the board, i.e. it must be executed during the flight, then the contrast is even greater.

It is also discovered that the greater the number of somersaults performed, the easier it is to increase the number of twists. During the basic Forward Header (a half somersault) it is very difficult to execute more than one complete twist. The same diver performing a Forward $1\frac{1}{2}$ Somersault will have no difficulty in including three twists.

Somersault Transfer From the foregoing it must be concluded that some of the somersaulting motion is somehow transferred to the twist axis. This is in practice achieved by tilting the body from its somersaulting axis during the flight so that a small amount of somersaulting angular momentum is transferred to the twist axis (Fig. 151).

The total angular momentum in the vertical somersaulting plane remains constant in magnitude and direction, but is now shared between forward rotation of the body about the lateral somersaulting axis and rotation (twist) about the body's longitudinal axis.

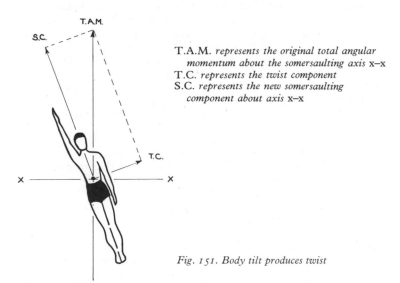

T.A.M. *represents the original total angular*
  momentum about the somersaulting axis x–x
T.C. *represents the twist component*
S.C. *represents the new somersaulting*
  component about axis x–x

Fig. 151. Body tilt produces twist

Effect of Body Tilt (*Fig. 152*)   Let us consider that a diver repre-
sented by a solid rod is somersaulting about his lateral axis viewed from
the front (a). His total angular momentum (rotational force) about this
axis is fixed in direction and constant in magnitude, i.e. cannot be
altered. Let us assume that during this rotation the rod is moved sideways until it is lying horizontally (b). The original somersaulting angular
momentum will continue in the same direction, but the rod will now be
rotating about its longitudinal axis. As the mass of the rod is now much
nearer the axis of rotation it will incidentally spin faster. Note that we
cannot alter the direction in which the mass is rotating from the forward
somersaulting plane.

Now let us imagine that instead of the rod turning sideways through
90° to the horizontal position, it only turns sideways, say through 45° (c).
In this case the rod would obviously continue to somersault about the
original axis and would appear as shown in (d) after the next half somersault, but it would be equally logical to suppose that the rod would *also*
now rotate (twist) about its longitudinal axis as well. Observation of slow
motion film confirms this fact.

Constant Angular Velocity   Only a very small amount of the original
somersaulting angular momentum is transferred into twist angular
momentum, but as the moment of inertia (resistance) about the twist
axis is small, the rate of twist will be quite large. As the body is now
tilted over, its moment of inertia about the lateral somersaulting axis is
slightly less so that the rate of spin is increased, thus balancing out the
loss of somersaulting angular momentum into twist angular momentum,
i.e. the rate of somersaulting (angular velocity) remains the same. In
actual practice the angle of tilt is very much less than 45° – nearer 10°.

All that remains to be shown is how the body is tilted and how it is
righted for entry. There are a variety of subtle ways in which this can be
done. These methods can be employed separately or, as in the case of
most twisting somersaults, used together and in conjunction with other
methods of twisting.

Tilt by Use of 90° Armswing (*see Fig. 92*)   When a diver with arms
extended sideways swings one arm downwards and the other upwards
his body will tilt sideways, the legs moving to meet the downward
swinging arm. This can be easily demonstrated by asking a diver to step
off the 5 metre platform with arms extended sideways then move one
arm up and the other down.

Tilt Produces Twist   As there is no angular momentum (somersaulting motion) present, there will be no body twist. If we now introduce

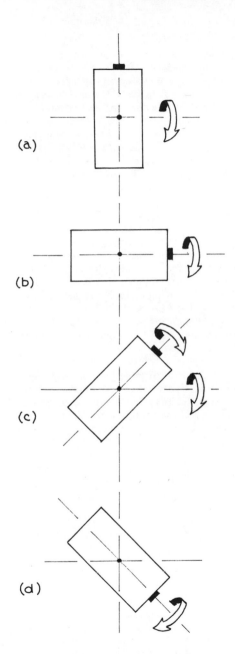

Fig. 152. Body tilt in theory

forward rotation by asking the diver to execute a 'dead drop' from the 5 metre platform, i.e. overbalance forwards to enter head first, the same arm movement will produce a twist. Experiments with divers performing an Inward Dive Straight proved this conclusively. Divers were asked to execute an Inward Dive Straight and place one arm in the customary manner above the head on entry but the other arm by the side. No mention of twist entered the instructions at any time. The results varied, but with most divers this arm action at entry produced a rapid half twist. The look of amazement on their faces as they surfaced was obvious proof that they were taken completely by surprise. The results were exactly the same when they were instructed *not* to let the body twist on entry.

Tilt by Use of 180° Armswing (*see Fig. 93*) Analysis of divers performing the 1½ Back Somersault with 2½ Twist will often show a 180° arm switch to produce maximum tilt which will, in turn, give a much more rapid twist. Robert Clotworthy demonstrated a 180° arm switch technique at the 1956 Melbourne Olympics during the take-off for his Forward 1½ Somersault with Double Twist. Instead of starting from a side spread position and swinging his arms through 90°, he took off with one arm extended beyond his head and the other by his side. He then switched the position of his arms by swinging them rapidly sideways through 180°, an action which would produce twice the body tilt and double the rate of twist.

'Wrapping Up' in Practice The so-called 'wrapping up' technique will not in itself produce twist unless the arms are moved in the 'frontal plane'. If the arms continue on *past* the body line at the completion of the swing, extra tilt will be given to the body and in consequence faster twist. The arms then usually bend at the elbows and are placed in any comfortable position close to the body's long axis.

Body Tilt in Practice In Forward or Inward Twisting Somersaults, when using the armswing method of tilting the body, the diver will usually start moving his arms as he straightens his body from the open

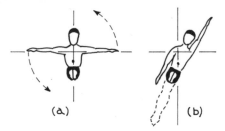

(a)   (b)

Fig. 153. Body tilt in practice

pike position (Fig. 153). The moment of inertia of the legs about the shoulders is very much less when the body is piked, and if the armswing is performed as the body is unpiked, the trunk will tilt through a much greater angle. The same principles apply when the body straightens from an arch position in Back and Reverse 'Twisters' (compare Fig. 153 with Fig. 92).

Tilting by Use of Shoulder Twist   Study of slow motion film, however, reveals quite clearly that divers are able to 'wrap it up' and produce fast twists without recourse to the armswing technique. This is achieved as follows. When a diver takes off for a somersaulting dive with multiple twist he will go into a 90° forward pike position for Forward and Inward 'twisters' or into an extreme back arch (in some cases nearly 90°) for Back and Reverse 'Twisters'.

Shoulder Twist Techniques (*see p. 149*)   Fig. 94 represents a diver in the pike somersault position just after leaving the board (viewed from the front). If he turns his shoulders to the right his legs will react by swinging to the left. He then opens out into the straight position and his body will have tilted sideways and this will create a rapid twist (see Fig. 95). This method of tilting the body can also be demonstrated by asking a diver to hang from the 5 metre platform in the pike position. He drops from the board holding the pike position, then turns his shoulders through 50° and straightens his body. He will be seen to be tilted sideways when viewed from the front. A good demonstrator will be able to do this from a pike jump. As, however, there is no rotation, there will be no twist produced.

George Nissen was able to demonstrate on the trampoline a Front Somersault with $1\frac{1}{2}$ Twists with his hands in his pockets, using his shoulders only to initiate the twist. The body tilt or sidecast observed in twisting dives was in the past considered to be an undesirable side effect, but in the light of present knowledge it can be seen as an essential feature of multiple twisters. When the required number of twists have been performed the tilt must be eliminated and the body re-aligned for the entry.

Righting for Entry (Forward and Inward)   With the armswing method, all that is necessary basically is that the arms are taken back to the sideways position in the *opposite* direction after one somersault as the body repikes for entry. With the shoulder twist method it is usual to swing an arm from above the head down backwards and sideways across the piked body to cause the legs to move towards the arm. This is done just *after* the body repikes ready for the entry. This final armswing technique is performed naturally by most divers.

Righting for Entry (Back and Reverse)   With Back and Reverse movements the number of twists is odd, i.e. $\frac{1}{2}$, $1\frac{1}{2}$ and $2\frac{1}{2}$. This results in the diver facing the *opposite* direction after one somersault. This will require him to move his arms in the *same* direction to eliminate the tilt as was necessary to produce the tilt.

Observations   With the body tilt method of twisting, the faster the somersault (more angular momentum) the faster the twist produced. It is difficult to perform a Forward Dive ($\frac{1}{2}$ Somersault) with Double Twist, but relatively easy to perform a Forward $1\frac{1}{2}$ Somersault with Double Twist.

Greater body tilt will also produce a faster twist. When the body is tilted, a twist will follow automatically and will continue without further effort until the body tilt is eliminated.

Conclusion   Most somersaulting dives with twist employ the body tilt method to create a rapid twist. The most favourable position to produce fast twists is when the body is straight and its moment of inertia about its long axis is reduced to a minimum by bringing the hands in close to the body. During somersaulting dives with twist it is the usual practice to perform the twist as rapidly as possible and as early as possible. Immediately after the take-off, the diver will straighten his body to perform the twist, then assume the open pike position to complete the required number of somersaults. It should be appreciated that when the diver straightens his body to the position most favourable for twisting, he at the same time puts his body in the most unfavourable position for somersaulting. This means that any somersaulting dive with twist requires *more* angular momentum about the somersaulting axis than a similar dive without the twist.

The expert will use a variety of twisting techniques performed automatically. He will in most cases be completely unaware of what he is doing. Any attempt to enlist his aid in analysing what he does is usually abortive, proving that there is a world of difference in what a diver does and what he thinks he does. All we can do is observe and try to understand in the hope that by doing so we are able to impart knowledge to those who follow us. In this way we may prevent time being wasted and so facilitate the learning process in the fascinating world of twist.

Index